The American Political Conservative

Your Personal Determination

To Preserve

Individual Freedom and Liberty

Jack Hamilton

First Edition November 2015

Copyright 2015

ISBN: 9781520671888

2

Introduction

To properly understand both the significance and the importance of accepting and wearing the mantle of an American Political Conservative, you must first come to grips with the meaning of Conservative. Unique to America, political conservatism involves the basic character of an individual and then the dedication to a set of core principles or values. Those core principles are so much a part of the individual that they are not open to compromise or dismissal regardless of the issue at hand. The core principles are the embodiment of the individual protection of each of the unalienable rights endowed on us by our Creator. It is the American Political Conservative who is fully dedicated to the furtherance and protection of individual personal Liberty and Freedom, essential to American existence. To understand Conservative core principles you must first understand the basic character of a conservative and the basics of unalienable rights.

Life is a sequence of choices.
It is the basis on which you make your choices
And how you deal with the consequences of your choices
That define you as a person.

Prologue

I have not always been an American political conservative.

My parents were born in the early 20th century, saw World War I as children, lived through the Great Depression, and were active participants in the efforts to win World War II. My parents were both die-hard Democrats. They believed that Franklin Roosevelt actually saved America from collapse during the Depression. They followed up their belief in a strong and powerful national government with near adoration for John Kennedy and strong support for the domestic policies of Lyndon Johnson. (In all honesty, I was a big JFK fan until I did a bit of homework about his actual accomplishments. It was easy to be taken in by the smooth rhetoric) They detested Richard Nixon, even before he was elected President, and thought that Ronald Reagan was the worst thing to happen to America in their life time. Had they been alive, they would have forgiven Bill Clinton for any and all mistakes he made and probably would have worshiped at the altar of "Hope and Change" created by Barack Obama. They were so wedded to the concept of a government solution to any and all problems that they could not and would not accept any other way. Their dedication to liberal democrat policies was confusing to me as I grew older and began to live in the real world. My dad was an active member and huge supporter of a large community service organization. He dedicated his later life to the service programs of that organization. I found it odd that on one hand he steadfastly believed that government was the solution to the problems of poverty and on the other devoted countless hours to fund raising and direct service to those in need. I found the two aspects of his life to be in direct conflict with each other. What I found even more surprising and confusing was that both of my parents were strong advocates of the very qualities that I grew to understand to be the basis of a conservative political outlook.

Despite my early childhood exposure, once I was out in the real world, I began to question and then challenge the political education I had received at home and in school. The initial hard lesson came in the form of paying income taxes on a salary that hardly provided sufficient funds for self-support. I questioned the use of the money I earned being spent by government on things I did not understand or support. My service in the Navy further strengthened my conservative outlook. There is nothing like having to live a life controlled by the political decisions of others without any means of speaking out. The ability to vote was sharply curtailed by at-sea deployments (absentee ballots were not quite as convenient as they are today) and there was little or no opportunity for political discussion in the wardroom or with contemporaries. Active participation in political campaigns was not practical and severally limited by law. Even with those restrictions, and perhaps because of them, my growth in understanding of conservative principles and my evolution to a conservative political outlook incubated. On departure from active service, I established an immediate active interest in politics, both local and national. I was living in what was then considered the most politically corrupt state in America and I was exposed to a brand of politics that was almost unbelievable. The local political joke was that if a candidate had not been indicted for a crime they were not fit to run and if not convicted they were not fit to serve. The local "election humor" was centered on stories of busses filled with voters visiting city cemeteries and recording the names of the dead and buried before going to the polls and voting in the name of the deceased. The stories were amusing but also far too close to the truth of local politics. Needless to say I learned a lot about politics and politicians.

After about 10 years in the land of political corruption, I moved back to my current home. I was really looking forward to a more genteel and honest political atmosphere. What a rude awakening I faced. In the 10 years that I was away, my small rural county had flipped from a strong conservative bastion to a liberal sinkhole. Because of the number of county residents (about 25 percent of the work force) who worked outside the county and used the county as a bedroom community, coupled with the 50% of the workforce serving in government jobs in the county, the flavor of the politics was closer to the nearby major metropolitan area than the mostly rural county I lived in. I continued my political education and my level of activity continually increased. Faced with the realities of an overwhelming liberal political outlook, I studied, joined the debate, and spoke out for my personal principles and beliefs. I became fully engaged in politics at the local, state, and national level. Through that experience it became reasonably apparent to me that the difference between my conservative views and approach to governance and those of my liberal counterparts were not the issues we supported but a more basic difference in the very principles and ideas that made us who we are. I came to understand that it is not necessarily what we perceive as problems and proper solutions but more how and why we make the determinations and decisions we make. American political conservatives and liberals are very different animals with different core principles and beliefs. Those differences are reflected in how we approach political discussion, specific issues, and the manner in which we deal with opposing points of view. Unless we understand those differences we will forever be at a disadvantage in the political arena. This writing is my effort to try to explain those difference and to set the tone for how we may better deal with liberal policies and arguments.

Please understand and remember that American political conservatives are those who demand adherence to our Constitutions and the rule of law and, in doing so, identify with neither the right nor the left of any argument but establish the firm center about which discussion may be conducted.

Table of Contents

Introduction

Prologue

Chapter 1   The Beginning (and the end)   13

Chapter 2   Unalienable Rights   19

Chapter 3   Language and Debate   23

Chapter 4   Conservative Character   29

Chapter 5   Individual Rights and Government   37

Chapter 6   Our Federal Constitution
             and Delegated Authority   39

Chapter 7   Concept of Privilege
             and Legislated "Rights"   45

Chapter 8   Understanding Delegated Authority   49

Chapter 9   States Rights   53

Chapter 10   Local Governments   59

Chapter 11   National Defense   67

Chapter 12   Foreign Involvement   73

Chapter 13   National Currency and Banking   81

Chapter 14   Transportation   87

9

Chapter 15   Commerce   93

Chapter 16   Moral versus Legal governance   97

Chapter 17   Addressing "Issues"   101

    A is for Abortion   107

    B is for Bullying   113

    C is for Crisis Management   115

    D is for Death Penalty   121

    E is for Economic Development   125

    F is for Free Lunch Lifestyle (entitlements)   131

    G is for "Gay" Rights   135

    H is for Home Ownership   141

    I is for Immigration   145

    J is for Jihad and The War on Terror   151

    K is for K-12 Education   155

    L is for Legislated "Rights"   159

    M is for Medical Care   161

    N is for Nanny State   165

    O is for Ownership of Private Property   169

P is for Prejudice (in general)   175

R is for Resistance and Assembly
    (Civil Disobedience)   179

S is for Social Security   183

T is for Taxation   189

U is for Uniformed Military Service   193

V is for Veterans Programs   197

W is for Welfare Programs   201

Chapter 18 Wrapping It All Up For Now   205

Chapter 1   The Beginning (and The End)

The further away in time we proceed from the reality of our founding principles that made us a nation, the easier it is to forget those principles and how very unique and important they are.

"In 1492 Columbus sailed the ocean blue" and made one of the most important errors in the history of the world. Instead of finding the fabled ocean route to the "east" he stumbled across an entire "new world". What followed was not always pretty or something to honor with great pride, but it was consistent with the politics and standards of the time. More significant, the colonization of the Americas is not a story of "rich white Europeans" enslaving and taking from "native" populations. Instead the steady encroachment of Europe into the Americas is a tale of unthinkable hardship, shared sacrifice, shared success, and a gradual improvement of the world as it was.

In retrospect it is easy to find fault with many of the actions undertaken by European nations, but it is difficult to separate the reality of the time from those actions. It was not just the Americas that realized the expansion of modern civilization; the entire world sustained a continuing period of exploration, colonization and turmoil. What is significant is that during the period from initial discovery until separation from English authority, what we now know as the United States was in fact an assemblage of European colonies under the rule and authority of European monarchs. That the American colonies survived and prospered is a tribute to the courage and determination of those immigrants who populated the colonies and pushed forward the boundaries of exploration.

A key word in the development of America, before and after the revolution, is "immigrants". Unlike any other nation on earth, America is a nation founded by and maintained by immigrants. Each and every person who came to our shores, regardless of means or method, has made an indelible and lasting contribution to the character and strength of our nation. That is a consideration we can never forget or minimize. We are not unique because of who we were. We are unique because of who we willingly became.

A fortunate matter of historical timing also played an important role in the creation of the American experiment. Across the world small numbers of political thinkers and philosophers were beginning to question the systems of government that placed unlimited power in the hands of hereditary monarchs and denied the individuals the same benefits of their labors enjoyed by a limited group of self-proclaimed "royalty" or their select compatriots. The Greek concepts of democratic rule and citizen participation in the governing process were once again on the minds of the people. Years of hardship and conflict on the European continent, with the ultimate price paid by common people, wore hard on those people and created a fertile ground for discontent. Actual revolution was precluded by an overwhelming strength in the monarchy and an inability of commoners to effectively gather, discuss, and plan opposition. In America, by fortunate circumstance, opportunity knocked.

The lack of a major standing British army in the colonies (they were busy on the continent and at home), the distance separating the monarch from those ruled coupled with the time/distance effects impact on effective communications, and a monarch and parliament buried in fiscal difficulties and constant problems on the continent, allowed American activists the opportunity to work together toward a solution to their problems. The initial effort was simply to gain the attention of Parliament and the monarch so that the colonies would be treated as equals to their brethren in England. The intent to actually separate did not take firm hold until such time as the government in England refused to listen and undertook actions more oppressive than helpful. In any event, the actions leading up to the ultimate act of rebellion demanding separation from the monarch's rule was brought about by men of education and understanding who possessed both the determination and courage to take the final step. While they certainly were considered to be extreme radicals by the English government and many of their fellow colonists who remained faithful to the crown to the end, they were actually, in the most part, sober men, committed to the concepts of equality and justice.

Our Declaration of Independence is a document of historical significance not only for what it did with respect to separation but also for the very foundation it established for the nation that was to come. Upon signing the Declaration, thirteen individual colonies, each with their own government and economic systems, embarked on a joint venture that offered no assurance of success. The Declaration established what we would eventually become as a nation, and why. The Declaration is the basic foundation of our nation as it exists today. The course set by the declaration was without equal in history, then or since. A small divided population of subjects, ruled by a foreign nation, having no central government, no army, no navy, and no treasury, told the Monarch that he no longer could exercise authority over them. While there may have been some hope that the Crown would simply act to resolve the problem through negotiation or simply not bother to respond, there was no way to ascertain the outcome on July 4, 1776. The die was cast, the message sent, and the future opened to absolute uncertainty. Only through an ultimate display of courage and determination, and perhaps the divine intervention of GOD, was the cause sustained and the thirteen colonies set free on an ocean of liberty. Unfortunately, as often happens in life, being set free does not guarantee success in the ultimate objectives. The colonies were free but the map and compass that would actually lead then to the future was not immediately available. Having earned freedom, the colonies now had to define what that freedom actually meant.

The trail from the victory at Yorktown to the ratification of the Constitution was a long and arduous path that frequently approached the brink of disaster. But for great fortune, the ability of a select few men, and the apparent hand of GOD, we would be a continent of mini-nations today. The ability of the founding fathers to try new ideas, monitor outcomes, and recognize failure was instrumental in the creation of the ultimate experiment that is our nation today. The Northwest Compromise and the Articles of

Confederation, though long forgotten, were essential building blocks. The lengthy Constitutional conventions, in which not all colonies participated, often appeared destined to failure. It was the wisdom and the ability to create unique solutions to recurring difficulties that saved the day. We now refer to the abilities of Adams and his fellow delegates as "thinking outside the box". They simply called it practical compromise. In the end, not even the most dedicated delegate to the Constitutional Convention recognized the miracle they had created or the course upon which they set our nation. Of note, none of the principle players in the Constitutional Convention compromised their core principles to reach agreement. They searched and successfully found ways to achieve objectives while preserving principle. Would that we could do the same today.

The efforts of the Constitutional Convention did not assure that the Constitution they had created would be accepted by the people. Even after a near disastrous revolutionary war against the crown and all of the propaganda against a despotic monarch, some number of the people were willing and anxious to return to a democratic monarchy. Individual states looked upon the creation of a "central government" as a sure sign of loss of their individual state sovereignty and another way to suppress the people of the state. Through the enormous effort of individuals like Hamilton, Madison, and Jay and their Federalist papers, were the debates carried and the Constitution eventually ratified. The Great Experiment had begun.

One of the main concerns of citizens in 1787, which lingers today, was the opportunity for a central or federal government to exceed the limits imposed by the Constitution and to suppress the rights and freedom of individual citizens. The first 10 amendments are the intentional acts of the initial framers of the Constitution to document specific protections of citizen's rights and the authority of States. While most people today believe they are "well informed" about the "Bill of Rights" few can identify all ten amendments or the content of each. Of all the "rights" contained in the first ten amendments, there should be little doubt that the restrictions on federal government imposed by the ninth and tenth amendments are the most often, and most egregiously, abused. Over time, since the Constitution was signed and offered to the people of America on September 17, 1787, and after the first 10 amendments were ratified on December 15, 1791, only 17 additional modifications have been made to the document. Because two amendments were self-canceling (the 18th and 21st) only 15 actual amendments have been ratified. In all, the success of our Constitution to direct the governance of a nation through times of peril and great success has been repeatedly proven. The wisdom and courage of those who refused to be denied equality and freedom set the stage on which we have played out our growth and history for years.

Since the adoption of the Constitution we have grown from a small nation east of the Mississippi to a continental nation with world influence and leadership. We have fought external skirmishes and wars to maintain our freedom and ultimately that of free people around the world. We engaged in the most horrific internal struggle to preserve the union and to bring an end to the oppression of enslavement of people. We have enjoined in massive political struggles to guarantee the equality of all citizens and have found the national strength to extend our reach beyond the heavens and into space. We have explored the far reaches of the planet and tried to bring health and a better quality of life to people of our earth. All of the good we have been able to do (and some of the mistakes we have made along the way) are but a continuation of the courage and dedication willed to us by our founding fathers. With all that has been a part of the American experiment, it would be only reasonable to acknowledge the United States of America as the first among the great nations and peoples of the earth. We may not be the best in the opinion of all but we certainly are the nation that sets the standard for liberty and freedom throughout the world.

With that in mind we have set the stage for reasonable and rational political discourse.

Chapter 2 Unalienable Rights

If "certain unalienable rights endowed by their Creator" are so unique and critical to the American existence, what are these things we call rights? Why are they so important to our American form of government?

A "right" is universal in application to all people. What is a "right" for one must be a concurrent "right" for all others. A "right" was endowed without cost or limitation by the Creator. There is no cost to any one person or group of people for a "right" to exist or be exercised by any other person. A "right" in itself guarantees equality among all with respect to opportunity but makes no guarantee of outcome. A "right" cannot be revoked or eliminated. A "right" exists independent of race, creed, color, gender, religious belief, or political conviction. In order to secure a "right" for any individual, that "right" must be first secured and protected for every other individual. A "right" is not dependent on being exercised by one or many to continue to exist. Neither government nor man can create or grant a "right". Neither government nor man can eliminate a "right. The sole reason governments are created by man, regardless of jurisdictional level, is to guarantee and protect the unalienable rights endowed in man by the Creator. So, what are these unalienable rights government was established to protect?

The "right" to life is the first and most basic of all rights of individuals. If we are to accept as truth that we are all individually endowed with certain unalienable rights by our Creator, we must, by extension, accept the existence and presence of that Creator. The basic elements of logic would then follow that a Creator would not bring us into existence as living beings except for the purpose to live. Logic demands that every individual must therefore have a right to life. The right to life is not a question of, or argument regarding, definition of when life actually commences to exist. Thus, simply stated, the "right" to life is the ability to continue to exist, as a human, without restriction imposed by or interference from others. The "right to life" is the ultimate "right".

19

The right to self-preservation is an adjunct to the "right" to life. Every individual has the right to take any and all actions necessary to sustain and protect their life and that of others. The right to self-preservation does not extend to denial of a right to life for another except in the event of immediate threat to self-preservation. Self-preservation entails any level of force or extraordinary action required to ensure preservation. To enable that protective "right", each individual must have the "right" to possess and employ any means and any level of action to protect their life from any threat. To that end, each individual has the "right" to obtain, maintain, and, when necessary, use such implements, devices, and equipment as may be necessary and appropriate to guarantee that protection. Any restriction imposed on the ability to assure self-protection is, in fact, a denial of the "right" to self-protection and, in turn, the "right" to life.

The "right" to self-determination. Consistent with the "right" to life, each individual has the "right" to determine and control how they will live their life. Just as they have no "right" to exercise control over others they must be free to make their own decisions, choose their own path, find their own success, and experience their own failures or setbacks. Each individual has the "right" to invest their life and energy in the pursuit of their individual dreams or goals. Each individual has the right to decide and act on their role in a greater society of man including the right to limit that interaction. Only through self-determination can an individual freely exercise the "right" to life.

The "right' of freedom of expression. The ability to conduct critical thinking generally separates man from most other forms of life. The result of a critical thought process is the achievement of conclusion and the need to express opinion based on those conclusions. Without the "right" to freedom of expression, the ability to exercise critical thinking becomes meaningless. There can be no curtailment of any individual's right to freedom of expression, regardless of means or media. Freedom of expression is applicable to all subject matter; political, religious, or social. The "right" to freedom of expression is not accompanied by a "right" to be heard.

You may express your opinion or thoughts but every other individual has the "right" to not listen, read, or otherwise receive or accept your offerings.

The "right" to exercise personal beliefs and values. One of the most extraordinary contradictions in our understanding of the concept of rights, is the ability of an individual to deny the origin of those rights without loss of any rights. While it was clear to the founders that there is a Creator and that all rights are endowed in man by that Creator, there is no concurrent requirement for an individual to accept or acknowledge the Creator. How we each see that Creator and associate our existence with the Creator is a matter of individual choice. Included in that relationship is the "right" to either accept or not accept that there is a Creator. Individuals have the right to deny the source of the very rights they would otherwise demand to enjoy. The very beginning of our national existence lies in colonization by individuals seeking relief from religious oppression. While religious freedom was not the basic intent of the early colonists (they were as repressive in their own ways as were the systems they separated from) they did set the stage for what was to follow. The early expansion of the colonies resulted, in part, from individual colonists separating themselves from existing settlements when religious comity could not be achieved. The "right" of religious expression allows each individual to believe and practice or not believe and not practice any associated relationship with a deity or superior power as they may wish. The "right" to exercise freedom of religious expression also embodies the "right" to speak out in favor of or against other religious beliefs or points of view.

The right of association provides each individual the unrestricted ability to share time and resources with others for common purpose. Individuals may also exclude others from associations into which they join. Individuals need not explain or justify their personal associations to anyone else.

The right to accumulate and own property. Individual freedom and liberty and the exercise of the "right" of self-determination can only exist when the results of individual labor and effort may be retained and controlled by the individual. Property, especially real property, is the economic basis for self-determination. Only through the "right" to acquire, own, control, and use property can an individual actually exercise any degree of control or influence over their destiny. Complementing the "right" to own property, is the need to maintain such property free from impingement or control by others, especially government, that would limit use or otherwise control value of the property. While individual owners of property may decide to commit to a use for the common good of their property, such a determination may not be made or imposed by non-owners. If the "right" to self-determination is to be protected, the "right" to own and control property must also be protected.

The right to determine and establish the authority and the limits of such authority of a government. If all rights are endowed in individuals by the Creator, then it follows that government, a self-imposed restriction on certain rights, can only exist with the direct and specific consent of individuals. In that no one individual has rights superior to any other or rights not enjoyed by any other, no one individual can exercise control over any other. Only through joint agreement can a system of government be created. It follows that, in the creation of a government, only those powers delegated to government, effectively the limitation or curtailment of individual rights, may be exercised by that government. When formed, the authority of government is detailed and fixed. Government does not have the ability or authority to extend or expand its scope or level of control. The various branches or departments of government do not have authority to determine the level of authority of any other branch except to determine that such authority does not exist. The only authority to expand or contract the delegated duties and responsibilities of government remain under the direct control of the individual who created the government.

22

Chapter 3 Language and Debate

This chapter may appear to be out of order. However, my initial editor, (my wife) properly noted that since the implications of language and debate will be strongly involved throughout this work, addressing those elements early on is appropriate.

Language

Over time, the primary language in our nation has evolved and changed. Where we once had a clear and direct link to the "English" spoken in England, we now have a language referred to as American English. In that evolution, however, we have not lost the basic meaning of words. The language of the Declaration of independence and the Constitution is as clear today as it was when originally penned.

Unfortunately, the language of common discourse and the language of politics are no longer common in definition or understanding. It has become acceptable practice to ascribe to common words new and unique meaning and to build phrases to create meaning quite distant from the words used. Over time we have developed a separate language with the sole purpose of misleading those who we address by using familiar terms to confuse actual meaning.

Some of the more pointed examples of language confusion are in phrases such as "freedom of choice", and "general welfare". In each instance, a political ideology has corrupted language to present a cause much different than the words would convey.
The term "freedom of choice" is normally associated as the rationale for the voluntary termination of an unwanted pregnancy. Of interest, the phrase implies that "choice" is the only appropriate manner to resolve a condition that exists because of previous choices and an apparent lack of self-discipline. The concept of 'general welfare" normally associated by proponents to the preamble of the Constitution, applies unusual meaning and intent to

that phrase. The preamble establishes the reason for the Constitution and states the following:

"We the people of the United States, in order to form a more perfect Union, establish Justice, insure domestic Tranquility, provide for a common Defense, promote the general Welfare, and secure the Blessings of Liberty to ourselves and to our Posterity, do ordain and establish this Constitution for the United States of America."

Nothing in that preamble could lead a reasonable person to believe that the intent of the framers was to create a system of wealth redistribution so that some citizens would become financial wards of the nation. The efforts of political liberals and progressives to redefine the word "welfare" and to create a system of social support for citizens has no basis in the Constitution and is directly contrary to the precepts of the Declaration of Independence. It should not be that difficult to remember that a principle reason for the break of the American colonies from England was the perceived wrongful extraction of American resources to fund English activities.

To make the point of changing meaning of words to confuse is best demonstrated by simple reference to a dictionary that predates the corruption of language. In 1958 the dictionary defined "gay" as "happy and full of fun; merry" with a fourth alternate meaning of "dissipated: immoral". That dictionary identified "abortion" as "a birth that occurs before the embryo has developed enough to live; miscarriage." and an "abortionist" as "a person who produces criminal abortions." An "immigrant" is "a person who comes into a foreign country to live" and "illegal" is defined as "not lawful; against the law; forbidden by law." There should be no doubt that those of our society who would strive for a major revision to societal mores and the role of government in our lives have resorted to corruption of language to achieve their goals and objectives. Perhaps more significant is that we, the conservatives, who are so dedicated to the protection of individual rights allowed the corruption to occur without positive counter action and have fallen prey to the curse of "Political Correctness".

24

Perhaps the most deleterious impact of the abuse of language in the political arena is the resulting inability to conduct meaningful debate. When one political ideology is able to so bastardize language so as to reverse meaning of common words and thus force their opponent into positions of apparent evil, debate is not possible. The ability to manipulate language thus extends to the ability to control discussion. Rather than being able to address and compare differences in core principles as applied to a question or concern, one side is relegated to defending an applied label that is contrary to their actual position. In essence, debate is eliminated. The problem is further exacerbated when, through continued manipulation of language, one ideology can redefine the actual meaning of general social concepts. For example, when a core principle concerning the moral approach to personal behavior results in being labeled as "homophobic" or "racist", it is most difficult to have honest discussion and debate. It has become common practice to simply apply a negative label to a competing idea and thus eliminate any need for consideration or debate of the idea. The process is now so deep seated that, in many cases, the ability to conduct actual debate is eliminated. More common to political discourse today is the application of negative labels and the use of short, fact deficient "sound bites" to substitute for actual fact based argument.

Debate

In any robust society which places value on the participation and contribution of each member of that society, the free and open exchange of ideas is a critical factor to the health of the society. If the society is, like ours, based on the concept that "all men are created equal" and that each has opportunity to succeed in life to a personally desired level, that society must also place value on individual ideas and provide opportunity for all to express their ideas. To be clear, not all ideas may be of equal value but all ideas have some value. The value of an idea to society cannot be determined until that idea is presented. In order to gain maximum value from each idea there must be a mechanism for the introduction of thoughts and ideas and for robust discussion, without personal rancor or off-hand dismissal. If ideas are the energy of growth and improvement there must be a means to assess all forms of that energy and bring the very best to the fore. Throughout history, open and fair debate has been the methodology of choice.

Debate, in its simplest form, is a discussion of reason for and against something. A proper debate relies on fact and clear language. While assumptions may be stated and employed in debate, they are never advanced to the state of fact without proper prior validation. The process is generally civil in conduct and those involved address the merits of the issue and not the character of the opponent. Proper implementation of the concept of debate is critical to the effective execution of the delegated authority of our government. The open discussion of matters of concern and the actions of our government are critical to the continued exercise of citizen control of our elected representatives. In fact, what was very difficult in 1787 should be more robust today facilitated by the technological improvements we have experienced. In reality, the opposite is true.

Far too often, today the art of debate to strongly support an idea or concept has been replaced by character assassination and emotional appeal instead of fact and logic. In Roman times killing the messenger who bore bad news appeared to be a common political response to that bad news. Today, in politics, it is apparently proper to destroy the messenger before the news is even delivered on the off chance that it might not agree with the position held by the one administering the destruction. It is also interesting to note that our society has grown so accustomed to the concept of character assassination that people no longer listen to the message. Too many people seem to decide between positions based on who does the better job of discrediting the opponent and not the basic ideas offered by the opponent. In politics, "hit" ads have become the vogue and are more important than actually determining what each candidate stands for, what their ideas are, and how they might serve the public. Perhaps even more alarming, there appears to be no reasonable restraint on the personal attacks. Truth really has become the first victim of political campaigns. In my home state of Washington, our Supreme Court actually ruled that candidates or third parties were not bound by concepts like honesty when addressing the character or positions of an opponent.

In addition to the expansion of character attack and misleading information now prevalent in most political discussion, the "sound bite" has become the normal means of expression. What started out as a general advertising ploy, the less that ten second jingle or phrase to link you to a product, is now the common manner to address even the most important problems facing our nation. Substance loses out over style and major concepts are addressed in "25 words or less." We, as a nation, have become lazy and have demonstrated a clear unwillingness to engage in even the simplest of protracted discussion to better understand a basic concept or to consider potential solutions to a problem We rely on forums (frequently called debates) in which a participant is expected to adequately address a major problem in two minutes. Even with those limitations most of us are simply not interested.

Without open, public debate of possible courses of action by government and opposing views on the proper way to resolve problems, we as citizens are guessing, at best, on which course represents our best interests and is consistent with our values. Public debate is critical to an informed electorate. If the primary right endowed in us by our Creator is the right to life then concurrent is the right to make proper decisions impacting life. To that end we must insist that public debate of opposing ideas is mandatory and accept nothing less. We must insist on civility in the discourse between individuals and reliance on fact and logic as critical to our decision making process. We must insist on settings that facilitate even debate opportunity, that all ideas be fully and properly represented, that all positions taken be fully supported by fact, and that any assumptions offered in support of a position be properly identified and considered as such. We must demand that ideas represent and address actual problems to be resolved and not self-sustaining "issues" We must insist that both the "Pros" and the "Cons" of each idea be thoroughly investigated and presented and that the opportunity for appropriate rebuttal is available. In the end, while the process of debate may not sway opinion or reverse emotion based decisions, the potential to support a decision or course of action on well-reasoned, clearly presented fact and logic will be available. And, if, in a robust society, the free exchange of ideas is critical to the growth and wellbeing of that society, the art and practice of debate is an essential part of that society.

Chapter 4   Conservative Character

There are a group of behavioral characteristics that serve to make each person a unique individual. More important, a number of those characteristics are common to most people, allowing us to function as a social group and to deal with one another on a reasonably equitable basis. Each and every one of us has certain needs that guide our individual responses to life forces and external challenges. Maslow completed the extensive research and analysis to develop both a schedule of common needs and a hierarchy of those needs. Within the basic and critical needs area, our actions are driven by personal survival. Beyond the critical needs level our actions become increasingly a matter of choice predicated on learned values and learned behaviors. It is in those areas of personal characteristics, above and beyond Maslow's survival functions, that we all develop that set of characteristics that define us as individuals and establish a predictable course of action for our responses to outside influences. It is within these characteristics that we can, through education and experience, modify our person and develop new characteristics based on gained knowledge. In our youth, we can mimic the behavior and actions of our elders to express like or dislike for persons or things. There is no inherited characteristic of conservatism, liberalism, or any other social and political philosophy. These are learned values that, in time, will come to shape who we are and how we approach the challenges of life.

I am a conservative. My belief system and those values that I hold most essential to my character and my very being are a combination of the values gained through continued participation in a free and open society and those learned through study and the lessons of life. If we are all the product of our individual life experiences, then there must be some other explanation for the existence of such diverse philosophies as those held by American conservatives and liberals (as well as other philosophical outlooks). Since most of us share an almost common set of general life experiences that would shape a philosophy, the differences we achieve must be a product of some other influence. In our current worldly environment the most probable factor for divergent philosophies is education, formal and informal, and those who would seek to provide that education. Regardless of philosophy, the underlying education must be based on hard fact and not assumption, to stand the test of time and the challenge of honest debate. Needless to say, it should be reasonably clear that my education has been offered by those having a more conservative philosophy. My conservative "instructors" have relied on fact and objective analysis to carry the day and have been successful. Unfortunately, when fact and objectivity are abandoned for the sake of apparent victory, the end result is not a victory but a shameful theft of glory at the cost of truth and logic. Such glory is false and will not last over time. My more liberal educational instructors, including my parents, did not abandon fact but more frequently relied on "feeling" or identified "intent" of historical actors rather than the more objective outcomes realized by the actions of those actors. In my conservative world, the reality of outcomes or results override intentions.

Each morning, when I awake and rise to meet the challenges of the new day (and continue resolving challenges of previous days), without conscious thought, I accept some very basic parameters of life. Without these inherent understandings of our world, my life, and that of those about me, would be far different.

The common denominator among American political conservatives is a shared set of personal characteristics. These characteristics, like conservative core principles, cannot be compromised or minimized. They are the basic definition of the conservative. Not unlike the characteristics that we have all come to accept as those defining a Boy Scout, the conservative has definable characteristics. Among these are personal integrity, self-reliance, personal responsibility, self–respect, self-discipline, reliability, honor, dependability, and courage.

First, and above all else, I am committed to the principle that all people, by their very nature are honest and that personal integrity guides their actions throughout their lives. I am astute enough to understand that some small number of individuals are lacking in this essential character element. There are individuals who would sacrifice their honor and standing among others for the sake of false gain through dishonest word or deed. Yes, there are dishonest people in the world. However, until an individual proves to me beyond doubt that they are without integrity, I will deal with them as honest and true to their word.

While truth is an absolute, the application of truth in a manner specifically to do harm, is not absolute. There is no mandate that we must always speak the "truth, the whole truth, and nothing but the truth" in every circumstance. This is not offered as a method to diminish integrity to a subjective concept but rather to place the adherence to speaking truth in an objective perspective. In some instances, silence may be the ultimate truth.

A conservative must be a person of unquestioned personal integrity. In our dealing with all others, and especially with ourselves, Conservatives must hold that truth shall be maintained and never compromised. The essential nature of integrity also requires that we will continually search for truth in all things that we deal with. Further that we will faithfully represent the facts as they are rather than as we might wish them to be. We will also hold that all others that we deal with have absolute personal integrity and will not alter that judgment until such time as an individual clearly proves otherwise. In our dealing with others, we anticipate that they will exercise a similar value system based on truth, integrity, and honor. The young men and women that we train to be the future leaders of our country at our military academies have an instilled code of ethical behavior that will not tolerate anything less than complete personal integrity. How can we accept anything less in ourselves?

Conservatives do not have a lock or unilateral embodiment on the necessity for honesty, integrity, and truth in dealing with all others, but those core characteristics have an absolute lock on political conservatives. Consider that open, meaningful discussion or debate over any matter of interest may not occur if truth and integrity do not gird the words, thoughts, and deeds of all participants. How can meaningful negotiation and resolution in any matter be achieved if full truth and honesty are not the essential element of the process? How can any individual be bound to contract or promise if deceit is a part of such agreement? How will we each, as individuals, find ourselves able to deal with all other in our day-to-day lives if we are unable or unwilling to assume the integrity of others? Do we not all (conservatives at least) automatically assume, without specific evidence to the contrary, that what we are being told by others to be the truth and reject the possibility of being misled by their statements? Truth is not situational, variable, or conditional. Truth is an absolute, and part of a Conservative characteristic that cannot be compromised.

A political conservative values and requires fact as a primary element of discussion and decision making. Sometimes it is hard to distinguish between fact and truth. Truth does not lend itself to comparison with other truth or analytical analysis to determine validity. Truth simply is. Fact, on the other hand, may lend itself to blending with other facts of like interest and subsequent analysis in order to properly understand the fact in context. At issue then is the nature of determining individual fact, the bundling of facts, the analysis process or methodology, and the final determination of the analytical results. In conducting research, conservatives tend to follow a scientific methodology that states the entering theory or hypothesis as a negative statement. Doing so places the extreme burden on the analytical process to disprove that entering argument and to support a resulting positive statement outcome. For example, responding to the hypothesis that "ABC does not cause XYZ" will require close examination of both ABC and XYZ. The assembly and analysis of all available and pertinent facts to prove the hypothesis will either result in such determination or an overwhelming body of evidence that ABC is the cause of XYZ. In comparison, a hypothesis that "ABC is the cause of XYZ" lends itself to a quick assembly of selected facts that support the hypothesis, without apparent demand for contrary evidence, and a simple analysis to achieve the desired outcome. Unfortunately the second process allows for easily contrived fact and, eventually, improperly validated conclusions that do not meet accepted scientific methodology. Like truth, Fact is. To accept that fact has been knowingly manipulated incorrectly or to fail to subject fact to the most rigorous analytical inspection is to be less than honest.

As a Conservative, I am committed to the principle that every individual is responsible for their words and actions. This commitment comes with an understanding that words have meaning and that actions have consequences. Each morning, as I brush my teeth and shave, the person I see in the mirror is the person responsible for my life. That person is the same old "me, myself, and I" that I have had to answer to every day of my life. Each day I remember from Hamlet a father's advice to his son "to thine own self be true." Of course, to hold all others to this standard of performance requires that each hold himself to the same standard. Those standards must be high. The standards must be, as all others, based on the initial concepts of personal integrity and honesty. The premise of personal accountability cannot be overridden by the actions of others to hold individuals to standards that do not exist or to create the impression of failure by creating impossible standards. In our current political discourse, Americans appear to be more than willing to engage in character assassination for the sake of gain than to truthfully debate real issues or analyze actual performance and outcomes.

In Washington State, the State Supreme Court handed down a decision that, in effect, officially made truth the first casualty of political discourse. The case involved one campaign distributing clearly false information about another candidate. The candidates were both of the same party. The Court determined that such action was permissible under the guise of freedom of political speech.

Unfortunately, for the citizens of the State, the decision simply removed all need for truth and, subsequently, the need for accountability from the political process. When government believes that it has been granted the power to support the use of falsehood and misrepresentation in the process through which political power is gained, it must also be true that there is no restraint on that government from acting in the same way once in power. Quite simply put, if there is no expectation that those we elect to be our representatives will ever be truthful with us, have we not created a system of government that actually rules and not governs?

A conservative is a person that values self-reliance as a way of life. We work to develop and maintain a level of personal capability so as to not require the support of others for our basic needs and requirements. This does not mean that we stand outside the normal bounds of society but it does mean that we will not expect that society to be responsible to provide support for our basic needs. Sometimes, the characteristic of self-reliance becomes a problem for a conservative. Since it is contrary to our nature to rely on others we frequently find it more difficult to turn to others for aid and assistance.

Conservatives are committed to the principle of self-discipline. Regardless of our willingness to be held accountable for our words and deeds, we have a personal responsibility to act with regard for others. What we think and what we feel are not to be controlled or limited by any others. How we express our beliefs and feeling should consider their impact on others. If the impact adds little or nothing positive to our life or to that of others, should we not question the actual value of those words or deeds? Words or actions undertaken for the primary purpose of enabling hurt or pain to others should be constrained by self-discipline. The Golden Rule has real meaning and serves as probably the best guidance for establishing self-discipline. While some believe that using a "religious" concept as a guideline for personal behavior is inappropriate, or even "unconstitutional", they would be in error. A conservative is self-disciplined. We know the difference between right and wrong. We will strive to always be in the right, to do the right thing no matter the circumstance. We are prepared to devote our very being to uphold right and to defend against wrong. While we understand that all of our actions have consequences we willingly restrict any of our actions that might do harm to others. We accept the responsibility for the consequences of our actions. We do not make excuses. We do not apologize when we are right. We promptly and fully acknowledge our errors. We take all appropriate actions to correct any errors we make. As J.C. Watts put it "Character is doing what is right when no one is looking." Conservatives have character.

Both good and evil do exist in this world. As a Conservative, I believe that I, and virtually every person in this world, stand on the side of good and against the presence or function of evil. That does not mean that we are all perfect or that anyone who engages in activities we do not support is evil. The presence of good facilitates opportunity for growth and improvement for all without restriction on any. Conversely, evil will only allow the benefit of the few at the expense of all others. Good is a constant force that serves to guide all to improvement while evil is an ever changing force that serves only to deny pursuit of good or to dissuade some from that pursuit.

A Conservative is reliable and dependable. When a commitment is made, it is carried through. We do what we say we will, in the time period we agreed to. We do not make promises that we cannot keep.

A Conservative is a person of unquestionable honor. Our word is our bond. The words we speak are truth and fact based. We will never forsake any other person as an expediency for self-gain or personal reward. We are bound by our honor to ensure the protection of the rights of all men. We will fight the fight for the disenfranchised and the downtrodden. We will never waiver in our character or our duty to all men.

A Conservative will not be limited in their ability to research or discuss items of interest by those who would impose the false constraints of "political correctness" on either thought or word. Conservatives will not allow themselves to be labeled an "extremist" or a "coward" because they seek to enjoin in discussion or to bring fact and truth to honest debate of a subject. To impose such limitation or to accept imposition of such constraint is to defeat the purpose of a society and to surrender a level of liberty and freedom won by the sacrifice of others who won for us the opportunity we have today. A Conservative will not dishonor or disrespect that sacrifice.

A conservative has great personal courage. This is not the kind of courage that has a person run into a burning building to save another (although that is certainly courage) but is the courage to stand up and defend his beliefs and principles against onslaught from liberals and others. It has been said that "An unspoken opinion is no opinion at all" and there is great truth in that observation. To remain silent in the face of wrong or evil is to condone the wrongs and evils. To speak out places fortune, friendship, and lives at risk. If conservative core values are not worthy of that level of courage, just what in life is? The prison that is created by self-imposed silence is one that is stronger than any an adversary could devise. Exercise the courage of a conservative and let your voice be heard.

While there may be some who will espouse conservative viewpoints or forward conservative ideas and principles but who do not possess all the characteristics of a conservative, there are none who will embody the essence of conservatism that do not display all of these characteristics.

Chapter 5   Individual Rights and Government

The most significant element of the "American experiment" in government is the very unique relationship of individual citizens to government. In all systems of government prior to the American Revolution, all power resided in a Monarch or central power authority and all citizens were subject to that power. The general concept was that GOD placed the ruler in the position of authority and that common people were bound to show obedience and deference to GOD's chosen ruler. It was always a bit difficult to explain those occasions when crowns were passed from one monarch to another at the point of a sword or draught of poison but that was the system. In our Declaration of Independence, for the first time in history, a people declared that individuals are endowed by certain unalienable rights by their Creator and it is the people who possess the power to rule and govern and not a monarch. While the concept turned the world upside down it also presented the most difficult challenge ever faced by a free people. How could a people delegate some portion of their rights or authority to a government and still retain all other rights and remain free? That has been a constant and ongoing struggle.

We live in societies that we have created to serve our common interests and to achieve some limited goals or objectives that we share in common. Our created societies serve us while requiring only minimal constraint on our individual pursuits of our individual goals. The basis for continuation of societies is the understanding that, as a society, we will accept and impose only those minimal individual constraints necessary to achieve the commonly approved goals. By the nature of our free society, those constraints must be clearly defined, strictly limited, and agreed to by the members of our society. An important condition to constraint in a free society is the understanding that any individual may defy the constraints of that society. However in doing so, the individual must also understand that the society has the delegated authority to extract payment or impose punishment for such defiance. The conditions of society that implement the behavior of individuals is commonly referred to as "the rule of law".

The universal duty of all government in America, regardless of level of jurisdiction or span of authority, is simply to protect and guarantee the individual rights of all citizens. Governments were created and exist for no other purpose. This is a critical element in understanding the role of citizens with respect to their government.

In the early chapters of this effort I noted that words have meaning and that men are taken at their word. In no case is that more important than in the understanding and application of the powers delegated by the people to our government. I would be remiss if I did not note that the delegation of power by the people to government varies with level of government and actual form of government. Our Federal Constitution and the Constitution of each state has clearly defined transfer of authority. At a local level a county or city charter will define the delegation of authority. In counties, towns and similar jurisdictions not covered by separate charter, the state Constitution normally establishes the form of government and the delegated authorities of the jurisdictions. For most of the United States the default form of non-charter county government is the "Three Commissioner" system, with responsibilities and authority normally identified in an article of the Sate Constitution. Of note, in delegating authority from one level of government to another, that authority cannot be increased or expanded and the delegating body retains responsibility for the proper performance of duty by the lower body. In the case of locally approved "charter" jurisdictions, the authority delegated to a local jurisdiction will be as delegated by the citizens. For sake of commonality and ease of discussion, we will deal with our federal Constitution.

Chapter 6   Our Federal Constitution and Delegated Authority

Our federal Constitution, adopted by the citizens of our nation in 1787, is unique in its brevity, its clarity and its content. That Constitution, in four pages of handwritten text, has changed the course of history in the world and served as the example of liberty and freedom for all peoples of the world. Oft used as the basis for creation of other governments, it remains unique for the courage and commitment of a people to self- govern.

Article 1 of the Constitution addresses federal legislative authority. In that article all legislative powers are delegated to our representative Congress. The concept of "legislative power" means that only the Congress has the delegated authority to create law or regulation for the purpose of government. That power is not delegated to or extended to the other branches of our government. Article 1 also establishes the manner in which Congress is formed to assure proper representation, the result of perhaps the most significant compromise during the drafting of the document. The House of Representatives affects citizen representation based on population distribution while the Senate provides equal representation for all states.

Article 1, Section 7 has the direction of the people that only the legislative body with equal representation based on population, the House, may initiate bills for raising revenues. While the Senate has authority to offer amendments to such bills and must, as a body, approve all such bills, the specific delegation of the authority to the House is a positive indication of both the intent of the people to clearly delegate authority and to make sure that every citizen was equally represented in matters related to raising revenues. Section 7 also delegates specific authority to the President, requiring his action to enable legislation passed by the House and Senate, demonstrating further the firm understanding of the limits on authority delegated and the checks and balances included in the

Constitution to ensure the limits on government authority. Of particular note, the sections addressing legislative powers do not mention the Judicial Branch, a positive indicator that the people did not desire or intend to extend any legislative power to that branch.

The actual delegation of limited authority to act for the people is contained in Article I, section 8. These delegated authorities or powers, as with all others, contain an understood responsibility to exercise the powers in good faith and to make no effort to exceed the authority delegated. Unfortunately, the unwritten responsibility has not always been closely observed and thus problems have been created and frictions caused between the people and those they elect to represent them. Once again the issue of "words have meaning" and the inherent integrity of individuals, comes to the fore.

In the Constitution, Congress is delegated the following specific powers. The words are taken directly from the Constitution. Plain English is used and interpretation to gain a proper understanding is not required.

"The Congress shall have the power to lay and collect taxes, duties, imposts and excises, to pay debts and provide for the common defense and general welfare of the United States; but all duties , imposts and excises shall be uniform throughout the United States;

To borrow money on the credit of the United States;

To regulate commerce with foreign nations, and among the several states, and within the Indian tribes;

To establish a uniform rule of naturalization, and uniform laws on the subjects of bankruptcies throughout the United Sates;

To coin money, regulate the value thereof, and of foreign coin, and fix the standards of weights and measures;

To provide for the punishment of counterfeiting the securities and the current coin of the United States; to establish Post Offices and post roads;

To promote the progress of science and useful arts, by securing for limited times to authors and inventors the exclusive right to their respective writings and discoveries; To constitute tribunals inferior to the Supreme Court;
To define and punish piracies and felonies committed on the high seas, and offenses against the law of nations;

To declare war, grant letters of marquee and reprisal, and make rules concerning captures on land and water;

To raise and support armies, but no appropriation of money to that use shall be for a longer term than two years;

To provide and maintain a navy;

To make rules for the government and regulation of all the land and naval forces; To provide for the organizing, arming, and disciplining the militia, and for governing such part of them as may be employed in the service of the United States, reserving to the states respectively, the appointment of the officers, and the authority of training the militia according to the discipline prescribed by Congress;

To exercise exclusive legislation in all cases whatsoever, over such District (not exceeding ten miles square) as may, by the cession of particular states, and the acceptance of Congress, become the seat of government of the United States, and to exercise like authority over all places purchased by the consent of the legislature of the state in which the same shall be, for the erection of forts, magazines, arsenals, dockyards, and other needful buildings; - And

To make all laws which shall be necessary and proper for carrying to execution the foregoing powers, and all other powers vested by this Constitution in the government of the United States, or any department or officer thereof."

In conjunction with the specific delegation of powers listed in Section 8, Section 9 places directed limits on the authority of the Congress in certain areas of delegated power. Section 10 specifies limits of individual state authority in areas that would conflict with authority granted to the federal government. Congress is also assigned additional definition of powers in other articles of the Constitution. Under article 2, the Senate is delegated the power and authority to approve treaties made by the President and approve certain appointments to office made by the President

Now, understanding the specific authority delegated to our federal Government in our Constitution, it is time to revisit that other document of maximum significance to America. The American Declaration of Independence, crafted by mortal men of uncommon perception and understanding, placed a heavy burden not only on the signers and those they represented but also on every generation of Americans to follow. When the delegates to the Continental Congress, representing their individual "states," adopted the words *"We hold these truths to be self- evident, that all men are created equal, that they are endowed by their Creator with certain unalienable rights, that among these are Life, Liberty, and the Pursuit of Happiness...."*, they did not intend that they be applicable only to the people of the time but that they would live in perpetuity and be equally binding on each successive generations of Americans. In reality, the proclamations of the Declaration of Independence remain as powerful and as meaningful today as in 1776.

The Declaration of Independence is the single document that clearly established that the "states" of America did exist as a common nation in the world, how those states came into existence, and established the manner in which Americans would govern themselves. The Declaration of Independence, with absolute clarity, established the supremacy of citizens over any government that they might choose to establish and that the primary responsibility of government was to protect the rights of each and every individual. For the first time in the history of mankind, the Declaration of Independence positively established that the authority of government was derived from the people and that government had no authority except that delegated to it by the people. In this relationship it is also clear that government cannot either through "interpretation" or in response to some immediate "emergent need" assume or take unto itself additional or expanded authority. Because of the primary relationship between citizen and government established in the Declaration of Independence, there is no manner or vehicle by which government can increase its control over or regulation of citizens without the explicit delegation of that authority by the citizens. The only function of government, manifested through the various authorities delegated to it by citizens, is to protect and guarantee the "certain unalienable rights" of the individual citizens. There is nothing in the US Constitution, the universal "law of the land" that modifies, negates, or revises in any manner the relationship of our citizens and our government that was established in the Declaration of Independence.

Chapter 7 Concept of Privilege and Legislated "Rights"

Children, especially those in their early teens, frequently claim a "right" to do something or to carry out some behavior. Most often the noted "right" has something to do with acting in opposition to instructions from parents or others in positions of authority. That they might be wrong never occurred to them because they have learned that concept from the adults who surround them. Never-the-less they are indeed wrong.

We all know by now that "rights" are granted by our creator and not by man or the constructs of man (read "government"). We now know that rights are unalienable (cannot be eliminated by man) and that they are granted universally to all. Rights tend to be major in impact and more global than the "rights" conceived by individuals to support their personal needs, wishes, and conduct.

What those young people and their misguided elders speak of when they claim "rights" are indeed either legislated permissions to do something or privilege granted for certain purpose. It is very important to understand the concepts because failure to recognize the nature of legislated permission and privilege will ultimately lead to an erosion of our actual rights and a loss of life, liberty, and the pursuit of happiness for all.

Government is an instrument of man established to protect individual rights and to complete those designated functions that are beyond the reasonable capacity of individuals. Governments are strictly constrained by the documents that created them and they have no capacity to grow beyond the limits established in their creation. A primary role of government is to self-police so that the boundaries of delegated authority are not breached and individual rights are protected. That said, it must be absolutely clear that government cannot establish or grant "rights" of any kind or nature. What government can do (and they certainly do it to excess) is to implement their delegated authority through law and, in doing so, create legislated parameters on behavior or personal interactions. For example, government can (and has) establish a central set of regulations detailing the manner in which contracts between

45

individuals and businesses are constructed and executed. In doing so, government has established rules of conduct for the participants. Purists will claim that government is infringing on individual rights in creating such regulations. They might recognize the error of their conclusion if they actually considered that a contract between two parties is a joint agreement to place mutual limits on their individual rights to gain a common objective. Individuals may always willfully place limits on their own rights. Other persons and governments may not so impose on the rights of individuals without the prior consent of those individuals.

Another often misunderstood "right" is the privilege of conducting some act that appears to be granted by government but is actually government carrying out an authority we have charged them to execute. No individual has the "right" to operate a motor vehicle on public property. Under our constitutions, we have delegated to government the authority to establish roads, bridges, and thoroughfares. In addition we have charged them with maintenance of the public safety on those byways. In the proper execution of those responsibilities, government has established a set of common "rules of the road" for the safe operation of vehicles, has established appropriate limits on the use of the roads, and has established minimum demonstrated knowledge and skills for individuals to drive on the roads. As citizens, in the interest of the common welfare, we have placed some minor limits on our individual rights to use the public highways. We can do that. But note that government does not have the authority to limit or otherwise constrain the operation of motor vehicles on our own private property. We did not delegate that authority to government and thus retain that "right" to ourselves.

Privilege may be considered as a process of generous accommodation from one person or group of persons to others. Privilege is individually granted, is limited in scope and may be revoked by the grantor at any time. Good examples are the property owner who extends the privilege of hunting on their property to certain individuals. Only the persons so granted the privilege have permission to use the land for the limited purpose and that permission does not extend to any others. The local Library is an

46

interesting case. In general, as a tax paying citizen, you have the right to use the local library that your taxes support. However, checking out books or other materials for use outside the library is a conditional privilege that is constrained with certain regulations and restrictions. Thus you have a right that is indeed closely associated with a privilege. The two should not be confused.

Back to the children and their claim of "rights". The "right" to attend school is actually a privilege extended by the government we created to establish a school system. The privilege is inclusive of specific requirements related to attendance, conduct, and performance. The "right" to privacy in "their" room at home is a conditional privilege extended by the parents. There is an axiom of life that goes along with children, parents, and codes of conduct. Simply said the condition is that "He who pays the bills earns the authority to set the rules." The number of incorrectly stated "rights" extends to the limits of the imagination of individuals. Fortunately, no matter how often many "rights" are claimed, they do not and will not pass the test of a "right".

Perhaps the most important reason to understand the concept of privilege and legislated "right" is to make sure that government does not exceed their delegated authority and unknowingly (or intentionally) infringe on the rights they were established to protect. Every legislative act (and more recently judicial decisions) must pass the litmus test of "is that within the specific authority delegated to government". This is especially critical with legislation that tends to grow based on prior legislation rather than initial constitutional authority. While governments may have been created to protect individual rights, it is the individual citizen who must be the ultimate protector of his rights and those of all others.

48

Chapter 8 Understanding Delegated Authority

Each of us lives our lives as individuals independent of all others to the degree we establish and can maintain. In reality, we are members of a number of social groups that allow us to achieve common goals more easily than we could through independent action. In order to make that possible we have to agree to allow the group to act for us (in our common interest). Such action by the group may not always be exactly the action we might take as individuals but it is the most reasonable action for the group to achieve desired ends. While acting within a group we do retain all of our individual rights and the primary interest of the group should always be to maintain and protect those rights. It is common, however, to personally limit the exercise of one or more rights and to delegate the authority to the group to act for us in that area. To be in our own best interest, the delegation of authority must be clear and strictly limited. Executing its purpose, the group must act within the limits of the delegated authority. The group does not have the ability to expand, modify, or extend the authority delegated to it. This is exactly the process that "We the people' have followed in the creation of our governments at the local, state, and federal level.

Concurrent with the delegation of authority is an appropriate delegation of responsibility. When we limit our personal exercise of rights with the intent of allowing a group to act for us we also expect that the group will act properly to achieve the end goals and objectives for which it was created. The responsibility for execution of the assigned delegated authority always remains at the uppermost level of the group organization and may not be assigned or further delegated to a subordinate level. While group leadership may further delegate authority to subordinate levels to complete certain actions or activities, original responsibility cannot be delegated. Certainly upper leadership or management may hold subordinate levels accountable for their actions, but they may not use that accountability to evade or diminish the ultimate original responsibility.

This concept is in play in government on a continuing basis. The US Constitution, State Constitutions (or similar documents), and local county and city charters (where they are adopted) establish the authority of each government at a specific level. Each of those documents is also supposed to include some type of "checks and balances" for government to be self-monitoring and to exercise self-restraint. Unfortunately, most of the provisions for checks are really actions that one branch can exercise to preclude another branch from intruding on their authority. There is little in any Constitution or Charter that actually acts to limit the opportunity and ability for government to expand its authority incrementally beyond that actual delegated. The control of expanding government authority ultimately lies in the hands of the individual citizen and is exercised through the ballot box or the court system. The ability of individuals to influence government action is limited, even when individuals band together in direct action groups. That said the pressure for government to remain within the bounds of delegated authority must be maintained constantly or tyranny will soon follow.

A primary example of the expansion of delegated authority is found in the rise of government agencies created to execute the laws created by Congress. In the main, the legislation drafted and adopted by Congress and the President is broadly stated as overarching goals and objectives. An agency, directed and operated by non-elected bureaucrats, is left to prepare and then carry out the specifics of the law. Although Congress is supposed to provide oversight for the laws they create, seldom does the oversight constrain the agency from expanding the original authority for the law (if there even was one). As a direct result of this lack of oversight and constraint by the legislative body, government agencies, and the executive authority guiding those agencies, too often find a way to expand and far exceed the original intent of the adopted legislation.

When referring to Article I of the Constitution, we can find the enumerated powers delegated to the legislative branch of our government. Section 8 of the article lists and positively identifies the powers that the states ratified as powers of the Congress. Over time the reading of Section 8 by the federal government itself (Legislative, Executive, and Judicial branches) has considerably expanded the original intent of the founders. The term "general Welfare" has been misconstrued out of all reasonable context to provide rationale for the federal government to expand into areas that were intended to be retained as the responsibilities of states or individuals. Those expansions, supported by Supreme Court findings and funded by Congress, now form the major part of our federal government and place great constraint on individual rights. Within Article I, there is no mention of education, individual health service, energy, or protection of species or environment. There is no authority granted for the federal government to exercise any control over any waterway other than ocean shoreline and navigable rivers. In short, there is no clear authority for the federal government to be involved in many of the areas we find them in today. It is easy to argue that "general Welfare" is the authority for wealth distribution packages and general health care programs until we recognize the fact that those programs impinge upon and restrict the individual rights of some for the benefit of others. Because that is contrary to the basic definition of a right and contrary to the primary duty of government (maintain and protect individual rights) it is also clear that such authority cannot be appropriate at any level of government. While the activities by government may appear to be in the best interest of all and to have a compassionate rationale for being, the reality is that those activities are not within the authority of government and to continue their existence is contrary to the best interest of each individual. Just because something "feels good" is not any reason to allow it to restrict the rights of anyone or allow government to exercise authority it does not have. The concept of "feels good" is not part of the Constitution.

Chapter 9   States Rights

The Preamble to the US Constitution starts with "We the people of the United States…" and finishes with "… do ordain and establish this Constitution for the United States of America." The crafters of the Constitution were careful in their language and used words to express a precise meaning. The terminology "the United States" speaks of a formal association of individual states (thus the term "united") created for specific and limited purposes. Nowhere in that preamble statement is there any indication that the individual states either considered themselves to be subordinate to a federal government or that they relinquished their sovereign status to a superior government. In chosing the language to close the preamble the choice of the word "ordain" is critical. The term means "to order by virtue of established authority." Through the use of "ordain" the several states clearly establish that they have the original authority to create the federal government for purposes as stated in the Constitution. The federal government only exists because the several states determined that it was in their collective best interest to establish a level of governance to complete certain limited functions not properly achievable as individual states.

In the event that there might be some confusion about the relationship between the several states and the federal government, the Tenth Amendment clarifies that relationship. "States Rights - The powers not delegated to the United States by the Constitution, nor prohibited by it to the States, are reserved to the States respectively, or to the people." In short, if there is no clear delegated authority in the Constitution, the power does not reside in the Federal government. To further strengthen the retained rights of the states, the process for amendment of the Constitution places full authority for such action in the states by virtue of positive ratification. The President, Congress, and the Supreme Court have no power or authority except as specifically delegated in the Constitution. With that fact in mind, there should be a clear understanding of the ability of states to constrain the ever present efforts of the federal government to expand and extend authority into new and different areas.

Seldom addressed in discussion or debate is the fact that there are two methods to bring amendments to the Constitution and for the individual states to exercise their rights and prerogatives as sovereign states. The most commonly understood method to amend is that of through the actions of the congress with ratification by the states. The lesser known method is through a convention of the states to amend the Constitution. Article V sets forth the manner and method by which a convention of the states may be called to consider amendments to the Constitution. The contents of Article V and the clear wording of the tenth amendment make it plain that the founders intended that the individual states would always have control over the authority and actions of the federal government that they established.

The process to amend the Constitution requires that not less than three-fourths of the individual states (that number is now 38) actively approve a proposed amendment through ratification. It follows that should one-fourth of the individual states (13 – that number rings a bell somewhere) do not ratify the proposal, the amendment fails. The same relationship should and must be true for any law or regulation adopted by the federal government that exceeds the authority delegated to that government in the Constitution. Should the Legislative bodies of not fewer than thirteen states actively object to any law adopted by the federal government by virtue of exceeding Constitutional authority, that law or regulation should be considered null and void. It follows further, that to avoid such a determination by the several states, any and all laws and regulations adopted by the federal government must have a clear path of authority through the Constitution. Instead of the lengthy legal process currently favored to challenge actions by the federal government in the federal court systems, a simple joint letter from 13 Governors to the President and Congress would resolve the matter. In essence, the states have a right to demand that the federal government prove clear Constitutional authority before adopting any law or regulation. Because such considerations will always deal with an unauthorized extension of federal authority, the suspension of the law should be in force until such time as the Supreme Court can find on the Constitutionality of the law. It should not fall to the states to have a responsibility to prove the federal government in error. Remember that the federal government is the creation of the people and the states and not the other way around.

Perhaps a couple of recent examples might assist in better understanding the critical nature of Sates Rights and the ability of the states to exercise those rights.

The first example might be "Obamacare" or the Affordable Care Act. Under this law, the federal government has mandated that all citizens must have some form of health care or pay a tax to the federal government. There are more than just a few problems with the law. The Constitution does not delegate to the federal government any authority to address the issue of health care. There are those who would offer that the act is covered by the commerce clause and they would be absolutely wrong. Nothing in that clause could ever be construed to delegate the powers that are assumed by the law. Further, nothing in the Constitution provided any power to the federal government to force any citizen to purchase or use any goods or service on fear of confiscation of private property through taxation. To the contrary, the law is directly contrary to the purpose for which the Constitution established a federal government. The immediate reaction by not fewer than 23 states to bring suit against the federal government over the provisions of the law make it reasonably clear that the states did not believe the Congress or President to be acting within their delegated authority. A simple letter from those twenty-three states with a clear "not gonna happen" message should have resolved the issue. Unfortunately, states have now come to believe that the only recourse to a federal action overstepping authority is to go to court. If that is the case, the immediate question must be asked "how does a federal court, created by the states in the Constitution, have the authority to override the will of the states?" It simply makes no sense. The US Supreme Court is a creation of the states, documented in the Constitution, to resolve matters pertaining to actions authorized under the Constitution. As such, the court cannot be a fair arbiter of questions relating to assumed authority on the part of the federal government. To better understand the lack of ability of the Court to be fair and impartial, the decisions of the Court to effectively "rewrite" the ACA, to a meaning that defies the clear language of the Act show clear bias toward the federal government regardless of delegated ,authority or the specific actions of Congress. The finding by the Supreme Court in the case of the ACA are clearly outside the bounds of court authority, contrary to the precepts of judicial impartiality, and certainly not in the best interests of the citizens of the United States.

A second example might be found in the actions and activities of the Transportation Department and the matter related to mass transit systems and rail systems. The Constitution establishes the authority to "establish Post Offices and Post roads." The Constitution is absolutely silent regarding manner of transportation or specific types of vehicles that might be used. None-the-less, the federal government has heavily "invested" in mass transit systems, light rail systems, and high speed rail systems. In fact, the government involvement in these non-specified areas of authority has developed into a very extensive system of quasi- extortion and coercion. Without any authority to dabble in anything other than roads, the federal government routinely allocates vast sums of tax dollars to non-road transportation projects. The key is that the funds only flow to those states and lower jurisdictions that comply with the various conditions and strings that are attached to the federal transportation grants. The end result is that the government levies taxes for a purpose not authorized in the Constitution and then allocates the funds to end uses having no clear link to any Constitutional authority.

A basic condition of rights is that they may not be lost or diminished if not exercised. Rights are constants. It is time for the several states to recognize that they have both the right and the duty to protect their citizens from excesses by the federal government that they created and over which they must exercise constraint.

Chapter 10 Local Governments

In the current national mind set, individuals seem to have greater interest in their government at the national level and much less interest in their local city, county, or state government. That is indeed most unfortunate because, while the federal government may get the press, it is the local government that has its hand most firmly attached to your wallet.

State Governments are a creation of the people (citizens) of the state. The authorities, duties, and responsibilities of the state are established and documented in a Constitution or similar document approved by the people. The state Constitution, similar to the federal Constitution, is a document that specifies and limits power. If it is not authorized by the people in the state Constitution, the state government does not have authority to act. Unfortunately, that association of lack of delegation of authority and the efforts of the state government to expand power appears to be frequently overlooked. Most states have a formal process for amendment to the Constitution and that process is exercised more frequently than at the federal level. Many states also include the right of the people to use the powers of initiative and referendum to modify the rules, regulations, and the state Constitution. It is indeed unfortunate that, when the people have reserved power to themselves, normally as the primary legislative power, the elected representatives spend great time and effort to minimize both the use and impact of those citizen powers. It certainly does make one wonder who is in charge and who works for who. For some reason the concept of limited government and restriction of power for elected representatives and their appointed staff bureaucrats has taken a back seat to the basic understanding that governments were created to serve the people and not to rule them.

Perhaps the most significant role that state government should play in the overall arena of government, is to protect the individual rights of the people of the state and to control and formally limit any excess of authority demonstrated by the federal government. If the federal government was created by the people acting through the legislatures of their respective states, and if the individual states have all rights reserved to them except as specifically enumerated to the federal government or prohibited by the US Constitution, the states become primary "watchdogs" over federal actions and excesses (Amendment X). The strength of the states to exercise control over federal action is also included in Article V which provides for the convention of the states. The ability to formally counter actions on the part of the federal government also includes enforcing the protections specified in the Constitution and clearly noted in the Amendments IX and X.

The powers delegated to the states by the people in their respective Constitutions will vary but, in general, they will address education, roads, highways, bridges, ferries, public health, policing highways, and other special considerations such as tidelands or rivers. The state Constitution also creates lower jurisdictions such as counties and cities, provides specific provisions for the conduct of those jurisdictions and sub-delegates authority to the jurisdictions. Common inclusions in state Constitutions are Article I statements dealing with political power, law of the land, and individual, or personal rights. In the State Of Washington the first three sections of Article I of the Constitution read as follows:

SECTION 1: POLITICAL POWER. All political power is inherent in the people, and governments derive their just powers from the consent of the governed, and are established to protect and maintain individual rights.

SECTION 2: SUPREME LAW OF THE LAND. The Constitution of the United States is the supreme law of the land.

SECTION 3: PERSONAL RIGHTS. No person shall be deprived of life, liberty, or property, without due process of law.

Those statements make it very clear what the intent of the people was in forming their government.

Unlike the federal government, which has become a full time endeavor and employment opportunity for elected representatives, state legislatures are normally part-time operations with time limited sessions each year. That does not necessarily mean that they are any more efficient or that the time limits the control they can legislate to themselves. To the contrary, because sessions are time limited and so much legislation is introduced for each session, the normal legislative "games" are played. Committee chairs decide which bills will be addressed and then forwarded to the full chamber for consideration. The Speaker and Senate Majority Leader exercise effective control over when bills are brought to the floor and the manner of debate. The political majority controls the process in each chamber and the end result is that few, if any, offerings by the minority party reach the floor for full consideration. The important issues like budget and expansion of power and control legislation comes from, and is ultimately controlled by, the majority party. Of course that is not what the citizens had in mind when the state government was established. For some reason, conservatives continue to look for free and open debate on a full range of ideas addressing solutions for real problems. Not all state governments work to that end. Of course, state governments retain the classic separation of powers with a legislative branch, executive branch, and a judicial branch. The intent of that separation of powers was to make sure that the guidance of the Constitution was followed. The short fall is that all positions are normally elected and even if specific positions are non-partisan the incumbents still carry partisan ideology.

County governments are a creation of the state. The "default" county government is the three commissioner form. The elected commissioners execute both the legislative and executive branch powers and, in some instances, act in a quasi-judicial role. In addition to the county commissioners, counties normally have a Sheriff for law enforcement, a Prosecuting Attorney to represent the county in legal proceedings, an Auditor for record keeping, an Assessor to establish property values for taxation, a Treasurer to receive and disburse county funds, and a Clerk to provide administrative services to the judicial offices. The names may vary and the actual number of elected may also vary but the tasks are common to county government. Recognizing that the various functions are assigned to different offices also helps us to understand the limits placed on the County Commissioner. Originally created to address the need for development and maintenance of roads within the county, the "Roads Commission" has evolved to general government function. While the primary responsibility remains with roads, county governments now deal with land use and land use planning, environmental protection, and building codes. In those cases where citizens have created separate taxing districts within the county for special purposes such as parks districts, library districts, fire districts, port districts, transit districts, and school districts, the county commissioners play no direct roles in those districts. County Commissioners may be assigned to "boards" exercising control over the activities of a taxing district. Because of the basic powers exercised by county government, the decisions by the County Commissioners can and do have significant impact on the operations and decision making of the special taxing districts.

County government has the most direct and telling relationship and impact on the residents of the county. If the county is operating with a central planning land use approach, the resulting zoning and land use ordinances will control the use of available private property for development and use. If the county is deeply concerned with ecological and environmental protection, building codes and other legislation will restrict the use of land, including private property, sometimes to the specific denial of all use of some or all of legally identified parcels.

County government builds and maintains county roads and sets the rules and regulations for road use in the county, including speed limits and traffic signals. County government has taxing authority to raise the funds necessary to operate the government, with sales tax and property tax being the two most common. County government also establishes fees for county services with building permit fees and auditor filing fees being most common. That said, it should also be understood that county government oversees the actual size of government in both expanse of authority and the number of "staff" needed to complete the government functions.

Not unlike the state legislature, county governments were intended to be part time efforts. Paid staff would do most of the heavy lifting and the Commissioners would meet, as necessary, to address issues that required their delegated authority. The part-time nature of county government also dictated that the commissioners had to be a part of the community making a living wage to support themselves and their families. When county governments self-expand to full time employment there is no longer any need for the Commissioners to be self-supporting nor is there any limit to the damage they can do using up what was previously spare time. It is not uncommon for County Commissioners to spend a great deal of time working with multi-county "coordinating" councils or with similar councils in the home county. While the concept of the attempt to "coordinate" common interests such as road development and ferry service between counties is certainly commendable, the actual result is not nearly so beneficial. Acting in concert, the multi-county councils have become the arbiters for disbursement of federal highway funds and similar federal disbursements. By joint agreement, the council makes "awards" based on the demonstrated "priority" of a particular project and the demonstrated compliance of the potential recipient with the councils "central planning philosophy". In the outside world the process is properly labeled as "extortion". Through involvement with the multi-jurisdiction councils, the elected representatives no longer actually represent the people who elected them but they become part of a larger, less accountable, regional government.

People have two opportunities to exercise greater control over the power assumed and exercised by their county government. The first, of course, is through the ballot box and election of conservative representatives. The second, and more difficult, is the development and adopting of a charter form of government for the county. The steps to a charter government are difficult. First the citizens of the county must, by a vote, authorize creation of a panel to prepare a charter. Then they must elect the representatives for the panel. The panel has a set time period to draft a proposal and present it to the people, Finally, the citizens of the county must vote to approve the charter. A charter allows for greater separation of powers, different criteria for electing officials, placing strict limits on the power of the commissioners (the power of the other offices are established by the state), providing for initiative and referendum in county government, and various other provisions. The intent of a charter government is that the people of the county are accepting full responsibility for self-government and the consequences of that decision. It does not assure that the actual government will be conservative but certainly the principles behind a charter government are conservative.

City government comes into being when the citizens living in a clearly defined area decide by vote to "incorporate" and form a city government. The process is not unlike the charter process for the county except that the initial vote is for incorporation. The city government can be of various forms and have a clear separation of powers. The duties, responsibilities, and authority of government are set forth in the charter. In larger cities it is more common for services such as police, fire, and general utilities to be provided by the city and to be included in the city government. City government does for the citizens of the city all of the things that were previously provided by the county. Much like county government, city government can expand without limit except as countered by direct citizen action at the ballot box.

The actual impact of local government is the very direct nature through which the rules and regulations adopted by those bodies directly impact the individual citizen. Certainly a state gas tax, which is purported to go to highways but is frequently allocated to mass transit, should be a major concern. Special funds created to support specific purposes such as a school fund that gets allocated to some purpose other than direct support of classroom education should raise voter ire. Property tax dollars that are used to create and enforce provisions that limit the property rights of any individual should promote downright anger. All of these thing happen at the immediate local level. Unfortunately, far too many people are focused on what is going on in DC to recognize or realize the negative impact of local government. To make matters worse, local government office holders are normally the source of candidates for national offices. Is there some reason to believe they would change their manner of approaching governance as they climb the ladder of success?

Chapter 11   National Defense

A primary purpose for the individual states to join in a union is clearly spelled out in the preamble of the Constitution: "provide for the common defense". The just completed Revolutionary War and the continuing turmoil in the world served as ample incentive for that purpose. Shortly after the creation of the Union the resolve for common defense was tested by conflict with the Barbary Pirates in the early 1800's and the war of 1812 with Great Britain.

In most discussion about national defense, the conversation normally turns to our military and the cost of maintaining armies, navies and air forces. Seldom does the discussion link the concept of international diplomacy and military strength. In reality, that link is the primary reason for a standing military and must be properly considered. The threat of, or actual application of, military force, properly invoked, allows the diplomatic effort of the nation to proceed to achieve results appropriate to the safety of the nation and its citizens overseas. It should be understood that military force is applied to bring the opposing parties back to the negotiations and to facilitate resolution of a disagreement. Without a strong military presence and the ability to project power, no country will long prevail. How much military, and what the proper composition of our military should be, will always be a question. That we have a strong military should never be an issue of debate.

Over the past few years much has been said by the informed and the uninformed concerning the "necessity" or the "right" of the United States to use armed force against Iraq and other nations of the world. While the discussions have been heated and provided great entertainment, neither side has properly applied the lessons of history to the current situation in order to properly assess the appropriate course of action. I have yet to hear either side cite the acknowledged experts on the subject of war (Clausewitz, Jomini, or Sun Tzu) as a national policy issue.

War is a matter of a state's foreign policy and the armed forces of a state serve only to further that policy. While war may historically have numerous causes or reasons for occurrence, there is general agreement that war is the logical extension of the failure of meaningful negotiation between political adversaries. In this instance, the armed forces serve to "buy" time for the diplomats or to force the adversary back to the negotiation table.

A number of international challenges over the past twenty years or so provide clear lessons on the purpose and application of military force as an instrument of diplomacy.

North Korea has been a belligerent and aggressive nation on the world scene since the conclusion of the UN "Korean police action" over 50 years ago. The dictator state has routinely threatened military action against South Korea and more recently the US. On several occasions, those threats have been carried out in the form of border incursions and military actions against South Korean naval forces. While relying on the military force of China to protect them from international military reprisals for their actions, the North Korean government is very much aware of the potential threat of that military action and walks a fine line between tolerable and unacceptable actions. The combination of economic sanctions and the threat of military action has brought North Korea to the negotiating table on occasion. However, that diminishing potential for external military action against the country has allowed North Korea to become more aggressive on the world stage. In this instance, the reduction in the significance of threats of military reprisal has emboldened the nation.

Iraq claimed to invade the neighboring country of Kuwait to restore that country and its economic riches to its rightful place as a part of Iraq. An initial effort to negotiate a withdrawal of Iraq military forces and to restore normalcy was not successful. Outside military action was initiated and Iraq was driven out of Kuwait. Because the objective of the military action was limited to restoring Kuwait, no effort was made to pursue Iraqi forces beyond the borders or to

68

conduct general war with Iraq. Instead, the military action resulted in a protracted period of negotiations with Iraq to bring that nation into compliance with international demands. The primary issue was for Iraq to cease actions that made them a positive threat to the other nations in the region and, specifically, to cease production and stockpiling of weapons of mass destruction. Over a period of several years the negotiations continued with Iraq playing the role of serious negotiator and radical state at various times in that period. Finally, based on international intelligence (actually not fully correct), a military coalition took action against Iraq. In this instance the military action was general war resulting in an overthrow of the existing government and military defeat of Iraqi forces. The creation of a new government for the country was also an outcome of the military action.

The Soviet Union failed as an experiment in communist government in Europe and the various nations of the Union were restored to their status as individual nations. Russia, the central player in the Soviet Union, while significantly reduced in power and potential on the international stage, remained a major world power. Russian efforts to restore Soviet-like control over some of the border nations have resulted in various local conflicts. Most were inconclusive. Unfortunately, most of the prior Soviet nations did not have the ability to exert significant military force and were unable to gain the international partnerships necessary to gain needed support in dealing with Russia. In 2008, following several years of political unrest, districts of Georgia along the border with Russia were struck by "separatist rebel forces" wishing to "reunite with Russia". A substantial part of the rebel forces were actually Russian military. The Georgian military quickly responded to the threat and promptly began to restore order to the region. Then Russia flexed its military muscle and entered the fight on the side of the "rebels". Georgia did not have either the military power or the allies necessary to stop the Russian incursion. The lack of international action to confront Russia certainly played a major role in the actions taken by Russia. Since there was no credible threat to force Russia to the negotiating table, they simply took the actions necessary to achieve their national goals. The end result was two districts of Georgia (South Ossetia and Abkhazia) being annexed by Russia. More recently, Russia carried out a similar "internal dissent" effort in Ukraine to take over Crimea and a section of the Ukraine adjacent to the Russian border. Similar to the Georgia actions, Russian "volunteers" aided local factions of Russian residents of the areas to aid in the dissent actions. Of some interest, it appears that, in part, the actions to "reunite" Crimea with Russia was in response to a Ukraine effort to more closely align with the West and potentially seek membership in NATO. Unfortunately, like Georgia, Ukraine did not have the military power to rebuff the Russian incursion and has apparently lost sovereignty over those parts of the nation now claimed by Russia. Of equal importance, Ukraine did not have the international relationships to prevent the action by Russia. Military force to mandate diplomatic resolution was not available and Russian military might worked to bring what will be an unsatisfactory but negotiated solution for Ukraine. The delayed interest by the western powers (NATO) proved to be too little, too late to have any real impact on the Russian actions.

Iran, in 1979 went from a pro-western monarchy to an anti-western Islamic state and began a long history of international political and diplomatic unrest. The creation of a major Islamic state power was not fully understood or appreciate in the West. When in November 1979 Iranian national overran the US Embassy in Teheran and took 66 American citizens hostage a major crisis was created. In this instance, because the Embassy was the focal point of the Iranian attack and the US could not exercise realistic diplomatic relations with Iraq, all negotiations had to be conducted through third party nations. The US was unable to press a military resolution because of geographical constraints, uncertain international reaction, and concern for the fate of the hostages. After 444 days the crisis came to an end with the release of the hostages but the alienation between the US and Iran continued to grow. Now some thirty odd years after the initial crisis, the US finds itself in a position of being unable to bring either effective military threat or effective limited economic threat against Iran. The ability to conduct meaningful negotiations with Iraq to achieve international goals and objectives is severely limited. The actions of Iran, throughout the conduct of negotiations regarding nuclear weapons, certainly demonstrates the lack of concern that Iran has about the potential of any meaningful military threat from the western nations.

International terrorism, most prevalent on the world stage since the early 1990's and growing to the point of open international conflict today, provides a new lesson in the linkage between diplomacy and military power. Through history, diplomacy has served as the tool of choice for nations of the world to resolve disagreements and disputes. Although not always effective as the primary tool, diplomacy has always been restored, even after military conflict, when treaties to end the conflict were negotiated. The process relied on the existence of nation states to serve as the parties to diplomatic efforts. The formation of the various "terrorist" fronts now present in the world, without a direct link or tie to any specific nation state, presents a major challenge to the concept of diplomacy and military force. The "terror" groups have no state with which to negotiate and, in actuality, have no desire to negotiate. These groups have made clear their objectives and have no intent to accept any other outcome. The remainder of the work is thus left with few, if any, options regarding a response to the threat posed by International terrorists. The actual options are to acquiesce to the terrorists and allow them to achieve their objectives or to counter their threat with a larger and overpowering military force to eliminate them. The use of military force has additional complications because terrorists may operate inside of existing nations and those nations must either join the fight against terrorism or be subject to military force from outside to counter the international terrorist threat.

The current example of ISIS/ISIL (Islamic State in (pick a country)), attempting to create a new Islamic nation (caliphate) from the territories of existing nations and to spread terror around the globe using modern technology, brings a completely new problem for exercise of diplomacy and use of military force. Historically proven

71

models of international diplomacy are no longer effective and new models need to be created. The one constant element is that the use of military force will remain essential to resolution of major international conflicts that defy diplomatic efforts.

All three of the acknowledged historical experts on the cause or rationale for war and the conduct of war (Clausewitz, Jomini, or Sun Tzu), are in agreement with respect to our current national policy and the manner in which the policy is being exercised. While an act of war may be classed as political in nature, that classification reflects the political agenda of nations and not that of factions within a nation, less they align themselves with the nations in conflict. Our current disagreements are not based on what political party holds the White House or Congress, but rather the national agenda of Iran, Russia, North Korea, and international terrorism, as opposed to the remainder of the world. It would be well for the "leaders" and "spokespersons" of those arrayed in opposition to our current polices to make themselves more knowledgeable with respect to the subject of war so that they might more properly assess their positions relative to national policies. It is just as apparent today, as it has been throughout our national history, that our national defense depends on effective diplomatic effort supported by an effective military presence. It also follows that effective diplomacy is only possible when a credible threat of military force exists. Without both of those elements, national defense does not exist.

Chapter 12   Foreign Involvement

There was a time in American education when every child was exposed to George Washington's farewell address as he left office as the first President of the new nation. That time is far past, much to the regret of those who understood the importance of the lessons Washington had learned as President and which he tried to express for generations yet to come.

It is frequently reported that Washington advised against "foreign entanglements" and opined that the United States should remain removed from the constant friction of the states of Europe. While Washington did caution against establishing permanent relations with any one European state, he did not recommend an absolute isolationism for the US. Washington's recommendation was based on sound reasoning. Prior to and following the American Revolution, European nations were engaged in a near continuous state of war or conflict. During the majority of Washington's Presidency, Britain and France, along with their various allies, were engaged in what became known as the Napoleonic Wars which were nearly global in nature. The United States, having close hereditary ties to both of the major warring powers, having small ability to provide meaningful assistance to either, and having significant concern about the economic impact of becoming allied with either nation, properly elected to remain neutral in the conflict. Even with that stance, the United States was impacted by both European powers through actions against commerce and impressment of US citizens into the Royal Navy. History shows that Washington was absolutely correct in his admonition against binding European involvement with a clear understanding of the probable negative impact on the United States.

As much as Washington was correct in his advice, that advice remains correct today. In a world that has seen two global wars, a protracted (and continuing) conflict of major ideologies, the advent of a true global economy with global impacts of local actions, and a continuing need for lasting agreements for mutual self-defense, the need for some degree of international agreements may be necessary, but the general concept of major binding agreements remains ill advised.

National defense, the primary responsibility of the Federal government, requires that the US link itself to like-minded nations for mutual aid and protection. Prior to World War I, the "war to end all wars", the US tried to establish and maintain the position proposed by Washington; remain neutral in European conflicts. Unfortunately, declaring neutrality and forcing the belligerents to honor that status are two different things. As the fortunes of war and international relations will frequently dictate, events transpired that made a continued stand on neutrality essentially impossible and the US entered the conflict. It is interesting that the US involvement, if based on public opinion, could have favored either side. It was only the specific actions by Germany that made continuation as a neutral nation impractical and brought the US into the war on the side of Great Britain and France. There is clear argument that the US was already supporting the British effort and that the US was not actually neutral but the actions taken by Germany overshadowed any arguments that the US was not a neutral nation. Perhaps the most significant outcome of World War I and the US involvement was the major shift of international power and the realization of the US as a major global power.

Nearing the conclusion of World War I, US President Wilson wagered his entire political capital on the creation of the League of Nations based on his "14 points" regarding international relations. Wilson had strong support from many European leaders but could not muster the support necessary at home to make the proposal lasting and effective. Because of the terms of the treaty which formally ended World War I, the near impossible economic burdens placed on Germany in the form of reparations, and the eventual impact of the global depression of the 1930's, the League did not endure and the stage was set for World War Two. Perhaps the single most lasting impact of the Wilson concept of normalized international relations was manifested in the dealings between

England, France, and Germany as the Nazi party came to power in Germany. The efforts to avoid war at all costs resulted in the rise of a national power that devastated most of Europe. The same can be said with the relationship between the US and Japan leading to, first, a Japanese invasion of Manchuria and ultimately full scale war with the United States. The lesson of avoidance of war at all costs and the unacceptable consequences of that approach were well established.

The conclusion of armed hostilities of World War II did not end the global conflict that continues to this day. In an effort to put in place an international organization to monitor and support negotiation between nations instead of armed conflict, the United Nations was established. Now, some 65 years after its creation, the UN has fallen away from its original mission and has become little more than a focal point of international progressive ideology. While the UN appeared to play a role in countering the aggression of North Korea against South Korean in the 1950's, that counter was a military response by a limited number of nations and not a full UN response. That the conflict was resolved with no effective change in relative positions from that at the start of the conflict and left North Korea as a continuing belligerent power, says little about UN power and a lot about the ineptitude of the organization. Since Korea, the UN has "dispatched peace keeper forces" to many places in the world. The effectiveness of those missions has been more determined by the belligerent nations than by the UN. In the most recent war on terror, the UN is missing from the battle field. Instead of world peace, the UN now expends major effort addressing issues such as global warming, population control, and human rights.

The US now is a party to numerous international agreements. Most of those agreements were the result of the ideological conflict that followed World War Two that created an international conflict between Communism of the Soviet Union and China against the nations of the "free world". The most notable common defense treaties that remain in existence today were the North Atlantic Treaty Organization (NATO) binding the various Allied nations into

75

a pact for common defense and the South East Asia Treaty Organization that binds nations of the region together. Over time both treaties have gained additional signatory nations and changed as the threat to the nations has changed. There should be no doubt that the existence of those major mutual defense treaties have played a major role in limiting armed conflict in the world and have been the underlying base for the economic growth and stability of the various nations who are party to the treaties. The US has also entered into mutual defense treaties with a number of other nations, many of which are either major providers of natural resources to the US or which are basically democratic in nature.

Unfortunately, far too many Americans seem to think that, because we have a mutual defense treaty with a nation or because we provide them financial support, they must have a set of beliefs and principles similar to ours. Nothing could be further from the truth and no single misconception is more dangerous to the safety of our nation. The United States is unique among the nations of the world in its understanding of individual freedom and liberty and the relationship of the people and their government. Some nations come close but none completely meet the American experiment model. Because of even the most simple differences it is a major error in dealing with other nations to assume that their self-interest and those of the US are common or based on the same principles. That is just not true. To think and act contrary to that basic fact is not in the best interest of the US, Even our very best "nation friends" have a different set of principles, goals, and objectives from the US and we must always expect that they will operate in their own self-interest. This is especially true when we are asking those nations to commit to a course of action involving military force and potential impact on their national economy.
To think and act contrary to that basic fact is to act not in the best interest of the US. Even our very best "nation friends" have a different set of principles, goals, and objectives from the US and we must always expect that they will operate in their own self-interest. This is especially true when we are asking those nations to commit to a course of action involving military force and potential impact on their national econo[JH1][JH2]my.

A good example of the nature of foreign entanglements can be found in the ongoing "war on terror" The conflict began a long time ago with minor activities by non-nation state activists (groups that organized and operated without the definition of national boundaries or internationally recognized governments).. This was a relatively new conflict on the international front. Previously, the approach was for states in conflict to attempt a negotiated settlement of differences. Failing to achieve agreement, one or the other of the states might enjoin in military action to force the opponent back to the negotiation table and to force an agreement. With the non-state activists, there is no state or formal entity with which to negotiate. Bringing military force to bear requires the consent of a foreign nation that, for record purposes, is not a party to the conflict. Thus the quandary of how to address the threat placed by non-state entities while remaining consistent with the concepts of normal international relations.

In the recent past, when Iraq invaded Kuwait, the US and other nations had a duty to respond because of existing mutual defense treaties. The treaties allowed military force to restore Kuwait but did not include counter invasion of the offending nation (Iraq). The action taken was to drive the invading forces from Kuwait and provide reasonable assurance that a future invasion would not occur. The conflict also resulted in specific "sanctions" being imposed against Iraq by the United Nations; specifically a number of sanctions involving weapons of mass destruction (generally known as Nuclear, Biological, and Chemical weapons). It was in this framework that the second Gulf War occurred.

On September 11, 2001 when a number of Non-state terrorist activists brought the terror war to the US, this nation was faced with a major problem. Prior terror attacks on the US Marine Barracks in Beirut, attacks on US Embassies in Africa, the first attack on the World Trade Center, and the attack on the USS Cole were all conducted by non-state terror groups. The US response was at best tepid and certainly not a clear picture of power projection and appropriate retaliation. It was clear that we had no real approach with how to address the non-state threat other than to try to find individuals and hold them responsible. That approach clearly did not work well. Following the 9/11 attacks, the US adopted a different posture that would hold nations either aiding or sheltering terror groups equally responsible and accountable for acts of terror. The first nation target was Afghanistan and the Taliban regime that was sheltering Osama bin Laden and his Al-Qaeda terrorists. The effort of the US working with the Afghanistan government to free the country of the terror groups continues as this is being written. The outcome of the effort and the eventual stability of Afghanistan and the elimination of terror groups from that country remains an open question.

While the effort against the Taliban and Al-Qaeda were being pursued in Afghanistan, the US noted the threat being created by Iraq in its refusal to be in compliance with UN sanctions and specifically those regarding the accumulation of weapons of mass destruction. The US lead a coalition of nations in the military action against Iraq. That resulted in the overturning of the Baathist regime, creation of a new government, and temporary resolution of a major threat to international security. In the face of coalition successes in Iraq, additional terrorist forces and support from outside nations for those terrorists (specifically from Iran) brought a new and different aspect to that conflict. In the face of a planned coalition withdrawal of forces from Iraq, terrorist activity increased dramatically and now a new conflict against a radical Islamic terror group, ISIL, threatens all of the progress made in Iraq and the safety and security of the nations of the middle-east and Africa. Unfortunately, the US and the nations of the previous coalition appear to have tired of protecting freedom and forgotten the lessons learned of trying to appease non-state terrorists.

Many have tagged the US as the "policeman of the world". That is a role, though unwanted, may be required of our nation. Edmund Burke is credited with telling us "All that is required for evil to triumph is for good men to do nothing". That simple lesson has been proven over and over again in the history of the world. We may not cherish the role of "Policeman" but we must accept the mantle of responsibility that has fallen to us.

We must first demonstrate the leadership that makes clear that violation of the generally accepted rules of conduct among nations will not be allowed without consequence and that no non-state group shall be allowed to function and bring conflict to the world or any nation without immediate and direct consequences. It is highly probable that US resources will be required to implement the leadership role. We must never forget what Burke offered us and what Thomas Jefferson made clear when he told us "the price of freedom is eternal vigilance".

Chapter 13   National Currency and Banking

Much has been made of the inappropriate power vested in the Federal Reserve System and the elimination of the "gold standard" in US currency. Both need to be better understood to properly establish positions relative to banking and currency in the US.

One of the specific provisions of the Constitution is for the Federal Government to issue and control the currency use in the nation. Prior to the advent of the federal government, individual states and even individual banks could and did "coin" money to be used in commerce. The difficulties experienced in determining the "value" of the currency of one bank against that of another or in having any real assurance that "coin" issued by a bank would be honored was relatively low. The lack of a central currency, backed by the full faith of the federal government resulted in an almost barter-like commerce between the states and foreign nations.

Two early attempts to establish and maintain a central or federal bank, strongly advised by Alexander Hamilton, came to light when the time- limited charters for each were allowed to expire. It was not until the late 1800's and early 1900's, after experiencing a number of national level financial crises and the attendant economic recessions, that the concept of the central bank was again considered. Even then, the inability of government to come to agreement in a timely manner delayed the creation of the central bank, the Federal Reserve System, until 1913.

While the federal government has the power to coin and issue currency, that is a function of the Treasury which was intended originally to serve as the "bank" of the nation. As set forth in the Constitution, all federal funds are retained in the Treasury and funds may be released from the Treasury to pay obligations only as approved by specific legislation. That system of banking would work well in a closed economy with all participants on an equal footing. Unfortunately, the international marketplace involves a large number of independent economies and monetary systems. Sorting out the relative values of currencies, one against the other, and assuring sufficient "coin" available to support international commerce exceeded the ability of the Treasury.

The Federal Reserve (FED) was envisioned as the national bank that would support individual banks in their requirements for cash and the ability to borrow money and control the amount of currency available in the economy to support the needs of the economy. The FED also acts as the central clearing house for checking and pays the securities and checks issued by the Treasury. The FED also serves to monitor and supervise regulation of banking institutions.

Because it serves as the Bank for Banks, the FED controls the interest rate that is charged for money borrowed by banks from the FED and controls the actual reserves (bank equity) that each bank must have on deposit with the FED. The interest rate for banks set by the FED (the prime rate) in turn impacts the interest rate charged by banks to their various customers. The concept behind the variation in interest rate is that in times of economic slowdown low interest rates stimulate borrowing and capital investment. Low interest rates are also reflected in low return on investment dollars that are left in bank accounts, so reasonable response is to get the money out and working. When the economy is booming, higher interest rates are employed to damp the enthusiasm and to prevent excessive growth. Perhaps a good example of the impact of interest rate on economic behavior is available in the consumer loans for cars and homes. When interest rates for car loans and mortgages are low, the activity in the marketplace increases and demand increases. Since rates are low, producers can also borrow money to increase capacity and place more units in the market place. There comes a point, however, at which the supply will far exceed the demand if not reasonably controlled. At that point production outstrips demand and excess supply is created. The producers are unable to sell their product and thus unable to pay their bills. A financial crisis is created. To prevent both situations, the FED closely monitors the economy and revises interest rates to exert control.

It is important to understand that the FED is operated generally free from direct political interference by the Executive or Legislative branch of government. The Directors of the Federal Reserve System are appointed by the President and require the advice and consent of the Senate. The Congress can exercise oversight but not control of the FED except through specific legislation passed by both houses and approved by the President. The FED is subject to periodic audit on some of its functions but not on the manner in which it acts to control interest rates or the money supply. Thus, with all the perceived evils of the central banking system, it is doubtful that our national economy or our ability to operate in the world economy would be possible without the FED.

The second part of this discussion deals with the currency issued by the US Government and how that currency is valued. Early in the life of the nation there was a definite understanding that currency was backed by actual precious metals and that paper currency could be exchanged for that metal (at a set exchange rate) on demand. The two most common metals used to guarantee currency were silver and gold. In 1900 the US approved gold to be the only standard metal against which currency was valued or could be redeemed. The act also set a standard weight of gold that would be the redeem value for a dollar. In 1933, in the height of the global major depression of economies, the US abandoned the gold standard.

The abandonment of a specific value basis for US currency established in some common rare mineral (gold, platinum, silver, diamonds, etc.) has resulted in a perception that US currency has no real value and that paper money is just that; paper. That perception might have some validity were it not for the fact that the lack of a material basis standard is now common throughout the world economy. In addition, obtaining sufficient precious metal to back every dollar issued by the government is impractical. With the understanding that currency amounts available in the market fluctuate based on the needs of the market, it is not clear how metal reserves would be handled. For example, during the Christmas retail period the demand for cash currency in the economy is at its peak. To meet that demand, additional dollars are printed and placed into circulation. Once the demand period is passed, the extra currency is removed from circulation. The value of the currency is not affected by the short term variation. The value of currency today is determined not by what it is based on but by what it will purchase. Currency has an inherent value to each individual based on the level of effort necessary to earn money or the cost of goods available in the marketplace. Thinking that it would be possible to refund a stack of dollars for a small bag of gold has become meaningless in today's economy. No one is prepared to deal in gold. In fact, fewer and fewer transactions are using cash as the medium of exchange, Exactly how does one get a gold refund for the cash value of a debit card or transfer gold from a personal brokerage account to pay a Visa or Master Card bill?

The fluctuation of the value/price of gold on the open market is another reason to not consider a return to the gold standard. If any one country can produce new gold at low enough initial cost it would be possible for that country to seize control of a major part of the world economy and dictate the value of national currencies. That would result in economic instability caused by production of gold (a reasonably limited use metal) instead of the goods and services that define standard of living. Holding gold would become more significant than any other contribution to the world economy. Wars have been fought for lesser reasons. In the world today the price of gold is not set entirely by the limited amount of gold available throughout the world. The actual value of gold is established by the demands of production of high technology equipment and the need for gold in that industry. While it is certain that some gold remains in vaults serving some level of basic security, more and more of the gold produced today is finding its way into military and industrial equipment and consumer goods. It is not clear how the gold in those applications would be used as a part of a standard or the impact such a standard would have on the total economy. One thing is clear however; the need to return our

84

national currency to a mineral based value has not been clearly established. The probability of the US returning to a gold standard, not endorsed and adopted by the remainder of the international economy, is highly unlikely.

Chapter 14 Transportation

One of the outcomes of an enumerated power that people frequently complain about but few understand has to do with the federal funding of roads and railroads. The complaints are not normally that the federal government has no business building roads but, rather, they don't provide sufficient road capacity to meet the needs of commerce and general transportation.

Predating the adoption of the Constitution, Post Offices were established and maintained in the major cities of the colonies. The Articles of Confederation recognized the existence of and need for a central post office system to effectively move the mail and personal communications. In the Constitution, the recognition was extended to include the power of congress "to establish Post offices and Post roads." At the time of adoption, several major post roads were in existence and functioning. Perhaps the best known (and still functioning today) to the people of New England is the Boston Post road which extends from Boston to New York City.   That road has, today, been incorporated into a broader federal road system.

With the advent of railroads and the ability to move the post more efficiently between major cities, railways became identified as post offices and the railroad track system became part of the post road system. One difference is that most railroads were funded by private capital. The federal government played a role in railroad development, especially following the Civil War, by granting large tracts of land in exchange for construction of railroads. While the federal government did not own railroads or system tracks, the federal government, through land grant and tax incentives, did provide incentive for the construction of specific railroads. Perhaps the best known of the federal grant constructions is that of the Union Pacific and the Central Pacific railroad companies that operated in competition for federal land to complete the rail line linking the East (Missouri River – Council Bluffs, IA) to the West (Sacramento, CA). The federal government authorized the construction grants with the understanding that the railway when completed would provide for the transportation of the mail, troops, war materials, and other public goods. Numerous other private railway construction projects added to a system that linked most of the major cities of America.

For those who wonder how railroads became post offices there is a clear explanation. In the early through late nineteenth century, and most of the twentieth century, most passenger trains operating throughout the nation included a railway post office car (RPO).

The original Post office cars were converted from existing freight or passenger cars and were later purpose built. The cars were outfitted and staffed to support the sorting of mail and the delivery of mail bags to towns along the way and to major cities on the route. Bags of mail were loaded onto the car at the point of origin of the train. Postal clerks separated the mail into bags depending on destination. Because the mail included monies and other valuable documents, the postal clerks were armed and prepared to ward off any attempts to rob the mail car. Along the route, at scheduled station stops, mail bags would be off-loaded for final delivery for further transport to outlying areas and new bags of mail would be on-loaded. For towns that were not scheduled stops, a special purpose Mail Crane was erected alongside the track to hold mail for pickup. The RPO car was outfitted with a "mail hook" that was extended from the side of the car, latched on to the mail bag suspended from the crane and brought the bag to the car for processing. Mail from the car was either thrown from the car or engaged by a mail hook alongside the track. Staff members manning the RPO were extremely well trained in the flow of mail along their route. They were required to have a detailed knowledge of the specific routing of mail to every location served by the route. They needed to know not only the towns and cities along the way but also the more distant towns and villages that were served through those route-side locations. The operation of the RPO was so beneficial to some railroads that the monies earned through RPO operations more than overcame the losses of routine passenger operations and kept the trains running.

With the advent of air travel, the understanding of Post roads came to include the facilities to process mail and transport it by airplane. That expansion of mail transport also resulted in some federal support for construction of aviation facilities and runways. Over time, as air transport capabilities grew and the cost and ability to move large quantities of mail between major cities or locations more quickly was developed, the use of air mail started to replace the dependence on the RPO. Today, virtually every commercial airplane in the sky carries US mail and the RPO no longer exists. Because of the dependence on air transport to move the mail (and for other reasons) the federal government remains deeply involved in the air transport industry. Of note, the insurgence of air transport of mail also had a renewal effect on the original post road system. Because of the impact of air transport of mail on RPO and the decline of RPO operations, the need for movement of mail over the roads from central airports to and from other cities and towns required additional attention to the Post roads.

Following World War I, based on some of the lessons learned concerning logistic support for deployed (overseas) military forces and the need to move those forces within the country, additional federal effort was directed toward both highways and railroad construction. The effort was substantial for the time but the impact of the great depression coupled with the actual limited need for a major highway system limited the expansion of the highway system. Following World War II and based on positive reflection on the transportation experiences of that conflict, both at home and overseas, the federal government established and commenced construction of what was authorized as a national defense highway system. There should be no doubt that the congress was authorized to fund that highway system under the national defense responsibilities or that the system was actually needed. How the system was actually built and how much "pork" distribution got in the way of the allocation of funds and the construction process is the subject of a different discussion. The now well- established system known as the Interstate Highway system certainly provided a much improved ability to move men and materials as well as provided for an economic boom and increased transportation "liberty" for the average American.

In addition to the federal government's involvement in transportation, each of the states, through their individual Constitutions, or similar governing documents, have some responsibility for roads and transportation systems inside the state. It is not uncommon for the state to have responsibility for roads and bridges that are of statewide significance. In states that required the service, it is not uncommon for the state to be responsible to support effective ferry service. However, that role is considered to be limited in nature because of the drain on the tax revenues collected throughout the state. Complementing the state role and responsibility in transportation, the individual counties, Parishes, and cities also have delegated responsibility. County commissions were, in general, established as "road commissions" and were responsible for the construction and maintenance of the roads within the county necessary for general transportation and commerce. While the role of County Commissions has expended over time, the initial responsibility remains as a primary responsibility. City governments have a similar responsibility for the streets with their boundaries.

Now, with an understanding of what the federal, state, and local governments are authorized to do by delegated authority, it is time to look at what they are not supposed to be doing. The current "hot" idea is for certain locations to build and operate "light weight rail systems". We all know that we need these systems because, after all, they work so well and efficiently in Europe and Asia. We are also told that by building these more efficient systems we will reduce our dependence on the automobile and reduce congestion on our roads. There can be no doubt, in cities where the systems were developed and extended as the city grew around the system, light rail works. Cities like New York and Chicago are good examples. The service is extensive (in the area served) and getting to stations is relatively easy. These are also cities that grew up with transit as a known quantity and development was arranged accordingly. The Washington DC Metro works because the station stops were created in the District and adjoining areas to serve the major locations of government employees or major tourist attractions. The system depends on those living outside the loop to drive or take ground transport to the proper station and then use Metro to do the major hauling. Because of convenience and the ability to get around the served area without a personal vehicle, Metro provides a viable alternative. That said, Metro has not had a major impact in the reduction of road traffic into and out of the DC area. The lack of Metro service to a wide variety of locations, the need to drive to a "park n' ride" lot to use the service and the problems associated with moving large items or a quantity of items via Metro make the car the transport of choice for many. And that is the same reason that "light rail" efforts across the nation have had a less than anticipated impact on the way people get around. Even skyrocketing gasoline prices (for America) did little to move people from their cars and onto "light rail" trains. By most reliable accounts, light rail and public surface transportation means serve less than ten percent of the worker commute for the nation and an even lower percentage of general travel. The costs of the systems for initial capital investment (construction or equipment) and continued operation places a heavy burden on available tax revenues. Of note, virtually none of the systems are self-supporting and rely on a continued stream of government subsidy to maintain operation. Of equal note, the federal Urban Mass Transit Administration (now the Federal Transit Administration) under the Department of Transportation lacks any authority to exist or operate under the Constitution. In reality, the FTA serves as little more than a clearing house for the distribution of federal tax dollars to states for a variety of transit related projects ranging from "light rail" or street cars to bike trails. The tax dollars dispensed by the FTA are in many cases driven by local jurisdiction acceptance of federal rules or restrictions that may or may not have anything to do with transportation, (The process is called "extortion" when a private citizen or organized crime employs the same methods).

The use of federal transportation tax dollars to coerce states and local jurisdictions into compliance with a full range of federal programs from central planning, environmental protection, and, most recently, "carbon footprint reduction" is clearly well outside of the delegated authority vested in the federal government. Only the most liberal interpretation of the Constitution, well outside the spirit and intent of the founders, could even imagine this expansion of federal authority. The overall negative impact on individual choice and liberty is immeasurable.

Chapter 15   Commerce

Commerce is defined as "the buying and selling of goods", especially on a large scale or as "the mutual exchange of ideas or social amenities". Certainly the framers of the Constitution had the "buying and selling of goods" in mind when they delegated authority to congress to "regulate Commerce with foreign nations, and among the several states, and with the Indian Tribes.

To properly understand the actual intent of the "commerce" clause requires that first we understand the meaning of Foreign Nations, several States, and Indian Tribes. Foreign nations are the easiest to understand because we can relate to those other nations of the world with whom we deal in international trade and execute treaties dealing with tariffs, import duties, product safety and the like. We control what we will allow another nation to import into the US and, in some cases, what US companies are allowed to export. We deal with each nation as an individual entity with sovereign rights and authorities and understand that we have no power to control the internal business practices of any country other than our own. By treaty between the federal government and the various Indian Tribes or nations in the US, those tribes have been recognized as separate "nations" and exercise sovereignty consistent with the terms of the specific treaty. The federal (or state) governments do not control the operation of the tribes or exercise authority over tribal lands. Tribes are not subject to all federal or state tax laws and enjoy freedom to engage in activities on tribal lands that would otherwise be prohibited on other private or public lands. Tribes or Nations establish their own government and control both membership of the tribe and the distribution of tribal assets.

At the start of the American Revolution, the thirteen colonies effectively became separate states (or nations) in the eyes of the world. Even though acting together in common cause, each colony maintained a separate government and individually determined to what extent they would support and participate in the war activities. At the end of the War, the colonies were formally established as individual states (or nations). Neither the Articles of Confederation nor the US Constitution have changed that international status. The individual states themselves have agreed, through ratification of the Constitution, that a federal government would be established to execute certain responsibilities that served the common best interests of the states. Nowhere in the Constitution did the states delegate authority to the federal government to deal with the internal matters of the individual state or have any sway over the internal conduct of business within the state except as specifically delegated in the Constitution. In addressing the application of the commerce clause, the federal government must consider each of the several states as an independent sovereign nation and act accordingly. Thus, when the states ratified the Constitution and delegated authority to the federal government to "regulate commerce among the several states", that authority was both specific and limited. In operation the federal government could prevent individual states from establishing laws or tariffs that would disadvantage another state in interstate trade. The federal government could prevent one (or more) state(s) from creating laws or regulations that would prohibit the business in an outside state from doing business in their state even though the business was legal and conducted in that state. The federal government could prevent states from establishing rules for importation of goods into the state that were more restrictive than the same rules for goods produced in the state. In short, the federal government became the agent of the several states to oversee and facilitate the flow of goods and services between the states. The commerce clause, as written, was never intended to support federal intrusion into the internal business of any one state or group of states or to expand the impact of government regulation over commerce in general.

Through uncontested legislative action, Supreme Court rulings, and Executive Order the original intent of the commerce clause has been relegated to the trash can and the federal government has continually expanded its regulatory and controlling powers over both commerce and the daily lives of Americans. By asserting that business actions within one or more states impacts the business of another state or the nation in general the federal government simply established controlling regulation. Food grown or produced in one state and either used on the home farm or not exported is still seen to impact the market of corn grown in another state and therefore a matter of "interstate commerce". The federal link is "stronger" if farm "subsidies" or federally controlled waters are involved in the production process. Electrical power produced in one state for the consumption of residents of the state also become a matter of interstate commerce if the fuel to produce the power comes from out of state or the power produced is distributed on a grid that has interstate connections. The combination of activities that would allow simple in-state business to be defined as "interstate commerce" is virtually limitless. In more recent imaginative efforts, the federal government has declared any use of federal highways or roads connecting thereto, waters flowing between states (or any waters connecting to them) or general air space to be part of the public square and thus subject to regulation under the provisions for "commerce between the several states". The number of rules and regulations currently in place and impacting our daily lives based on some tenuous link to the commerce clause is substantial and growing. Airlines, railways, trucking companies, barge and towboat operations, riverboats, fishing operations, and similar are all subject to federal regulation and control with links to the commerce clause.

There can be no doubt, in reading the US Constitution, that the application of the "commerce clause" to exert federal control over the operations of the several states and individuals has far exceeded that intended by the framers. The extended application of the commerce powers of the federal government is also directly contrary to the protections of the ninth and tenth amendments and the specific protections for life, limb and property protected under the Fifth Amendment. The Preamble of the Bill of Rights clearly identifies the concerns of the framers about the potential for uncontrolled expansion of powers by the newly formed federal government. That Preamble states "The Conventions of a number of The States, having at the time of their adopting the Constitution, expressed a desire, in order to prevent misconstruction or abuse of

95

its powers, that further declaratory and restrictive clauses should be added: And as extending the ground of public confidence in the Government, will best ensure the beneficent ends of its institution." Perhaps it is unfortunate that the same eagerness to expand power and personal control over the lives of people has become normal in our individual state legislatures. The very institutions that we empowered to exercise control over and limit the expansion of federal power are emboldened and supported by federal actions to enjoy similar opportunities for extension of power at the state and local level.

Chapter 16   Moral vs Legal Governance

Early on in my time in open society I was told that it was possible to legislate conduct but there was no way to legislate morality. After some considerable thought and more experience than I choose to share, it has become very evident that the advice was correct. Unfortunately, there is some portion of our population that does not understand and accept the basic premise of the caution. If it was possible to legislate and enforce a common morality there would be little need for government, or police, or any other legislative effort to dictate behavior. This is a difficult issue to address because some believe that the responsibility of government is to enforce their morality on all others. Sorry, it just does not work that way.

Moral behavior is a calling to perform in a set manner regardless of conditions or situations. It is the demonstration through action of a clear understanding of good and evil and always selecting good. In the words of J.C. Watts it is "doing what is right when nobody is watching". Moral behavior is not predicated on the possible retribution of a higher power although the nature of morality may have been established by that higher power.

Nowhere in the US Constitution or that of the several states will you find any authority delegated to government to establish a set of "moral" standards that all must live by and which will serve as the basis for all legislative acts. Legislation is used to direct specific behaviors of the individuals who are subject to the legislation. Prime examples are laws addressing criminal behavior, laws regarding operation of motor vehicles, and laws regarding the making of contracts. We live with these laws every day of our lives and consider them to be "normal". They are, purportedly, the "rules" that a society has established for effective operation and in the common good. Although many would argue that laws have a moral basis, it would be hard to substantiate that as fact. For example, if the law against stealing is based on morality, only those who are immoral would violate the law. That being the case, we could simply extend that a moral person would never violate any law and by default make society a safer place to live by eliminating anyone who broke any law. After all, if breaking one law is immoral, it follows that the law breaker is not a moral person and will not abide by any of the rules of society. Following that faulty logic would allow us to rid ourselves of all immoral, and thus evil, people and make the world safe for all. We should be glad that it does not work quite that way.

Remaining in compliance with the law and rules of society is a continuing matter of choice between common good and personal interest. People who either abide by the rules or break the rules do so as a matter of choice. They balance their own self-good with their concept of morality and their regard for the common good. The person who elects to violate a speed limit (let all who have not done so please leave the room), does so as a matter of choice. The decision does not involve a lengthy consideration of the morality of the matter because, in most cases, there is no perception of violating personal morality by going over the speed limit. Under the most severe consideration, the act is contrary to absolute moral behavior which accepts no deviation. However, the decision to willingly violate the rules opens the door to others who would choose to ignore other rules. Therein lies the real problem and therein also rests the basic reason for a society to assure the protection of individual rights and general public safety with as few rules as possible.

No one of us has been blessed (or cursed) with the "right" to decide which laws and rules shall be applicable to ourselves and which to all others. When I violate any one rule of societal behavior, I weaken the strength and reason-in-being for every other rule. If I actually believe that I can ignore a law and not suffer consequences of that decision, how can I hold any other person accountable for their violations? Thus, once again, the concept of morality enters the picture of law and regulation. Without a moral society, rules only apply to those who wish to follow them and have no meaning or consequence for any others. Under those circumstances the rules of nature and the simple principle of survival of the fittest becomes paramount. There are no rules, right and wrong are defined by each individual, the conduct of each person is without limit and society ceases to exist. Even in the absolute instance of a "society" without law, there actually is law except that it is imposed by the strongest on all others and maintained by absolute force.

Which then brings us to the second reason law and regulation can work in a moral society but not in a society with no moral underpinnings. When we accept that life is a series of choices and that every choice has a result or consequences, we also link personal responsibility with choice. That link is actual only when an underlying moral basis exists. Without any moral conviction or understanding results and consequences could just as easily be ignored as accepted. However, in the effective society, a choice that violates a law or rule carries with it the approval of society to extract any retribution or punishment that may be associated with the violation, When I break the law and violate the speed limit, I do so with the full understanding and acceptance that society has set a cost for that poor behavior. I may not be happy when Officer Friendly stops me and informs me that the cost of my digression is significant, but I have no option but to accept that conclusion. The same is true of an individual who violates the more significant rules of society dealing with life and property. While our social etiquette in resolving matters of violation of law provides clear protections for the accused and places the burden of proof on society, the bottom line truly is "if you done the crime, you do the time".

Having come full circle in the discussion it is very clear that while there is no way to legislate morality, a system of laws and rules to operate an effective society must be based on the assumption that the society has a moral basis. If you still wonder about the relationship, simply compare the social rules of any developed western nation and those of countries or nations still ruled by tribal groups or strict religious principle. The differences will be immediately clear unless you believe that stoning a woman to death for being seen in public without a veil, or mutilating the bodies of women and children is an acceptable way of assuring compliance with "law".

99

Chapter 17   Addressing "Issues"

In the world of American politics, it has become common , at all levels of government, to label the hopes, dreams, wants, and needs of the voting public in terms of "Issues". Through the use of the "issues" approach, political figures are free and able to not deal with those pesky concerns of authorities of government, cost associated with resolving an "issue", and the concept of authority and priority of government. Dealing with "issues" also allows politicians to avoid addressing the importance of an "issue" as compared to all of the actual mandated and valid requirements of government. Last, but not least, in addressing "issues", the political figures rarely are required to identify the source of the assets that will be required to resolve the "issue". That part is really convenient, keeping in mind that all of the assets of government were first the private property and assets of individual citizens.

Political discussions of "issues" are normally based on a limited selection of facts (obviously only those that enhance the importance of the "issue" as being presented) and a heavy stress on emotional response rather than a logical decision making process. More often than not, identified "issues" are not actually the real problems requiring immediate action but are only symptoms of deeper, underlying problems. Seldom does addressing the "issue" and implementing the solution offered by the political champion, actually constitute constructive, conclusive action. More common is that the proposed solution for an "issue" simply sets the stage for several new "issues" to be resolved.

The understanding of how "issues" are created and evolve to have a continuing life of their own was brought to my immediate attention during a visit to my local tire store to get my "winter treads" put on my car. While this example may be specific to one "issue", the concept of issue creation is common to most all.

To understand the nature of the "issues" in this example, we need a bit of background information first. In my early days as a driver, my car was outfitted with tires that required the use of an inflatable inner tube. Any puncture or even severe impact on the tire would result in a flat or a "blowout". At higher speeds, sudden deflation of a tire resulted in an immediate handling problem for the driver. Industry recognized the nature of the problem and the result was the "puncture-proof, self-sealing" tire. Later the concept was combined with a better design of the tires internal support system. Originally offered as optional equipment on cars, the self-sealing tire soon became a standard item. The engineering advancement seemed to fit into federal government concerns about automobile safety and increased gas mileage and making self-sealing tires standard equipment became an "issue". To resolve the "issue" a series of federal regulations were created and imposed on both industry and private citizens. You might question just where in the Constitution authority was delegated to the federal government to create regulations regarding automobile tires and your question would be a good one.

Subsequent to making the tires a requirement under federal regulation, self-sealing tires were tracked by a variety of manufacturer required data and could be associated from point of origin to a particular vehicle. All the better to make sure that the regulations were being followed.

In the late 1990s a series of accidents were tracked back to a single tire manufacturer when the cause of the accidents was determined to be under-inflation of the tires. Because there was no record of the care and feeding of tires provided by vehicle owners, the actual cause of the under-inflation was hard to determine. However, government regulators were able to positively identify under-inflation as the cause and an "issue" was created. How could government protect car owners from the hazards of under-inflated tires. You might question how a manufacturing error by one company gave cause to impose new regulations on all companies. That of course would only identify your lack of understanding of the "issues" process and the ability of government to expand authority using "issues". If you were naive enough to think that imposing more stringent design and inspection requirements for tire manufacture would be sufficient, shame on you.

The very fact that self-sealing tires could still suffer from under-inflation, coupled with the advent of new engineering technology and innovation in the open market, established a basis for a new "issue". The new technology, developed in Europe and destined for top of the line model cars, was the Tire Pressure Monitoring System which presented warning of tire under-inflation to the driver as a dash board warning signal. That the system was available and might prevent an accident was sufficient for a new "issue" to come before the people. Arguing public safety and availability of an answer, politicians, urged on by automobile insurance companies, pushed for additional regulation. Never questioning the actual value added to automobile safety by the new system, the actual need for the system, or the cost of the new requirement that would be passed to car owners, the political solution for the "issue" was to adopt regulation requiring installation in all cars as of September 2007. In addition to the safety aspect touted as a reason for adoption, a government study determined that under-inflation decreased gas mileage and that was bad for the environment. How could anyone possibly object to something that increases protection and saves Polar Bears at the same time?

Now that we have addressed the historical progress of issues relating to automobile tire safety (and an apparent significant expansion of federal government authority over citizen rights and freedom) it is time to return to the story of cars, "winter treads", and "issues". In some areas of the country weather patterns are actually defined by season related to the relationship of the earth to our sun. Some areas have a season called winter that is best identified by accumulations of snow and the occasional presence of ice on roads. To increase traction under winter conditions, drivers frequently install "snow tires" designed to meet the winter conditions. Because one of the down sides of self-sealing tires is that breaking the seal between the tire and the wheel rim is not good for the life of the tire, it is not uncommon for drivers to mount snow tires on a separate set of wheels. In doing so, those thoughtful drivers have created another "issue" and fallen afoul of political thinking.

Because the Tire Pressure Monitoring System (TPMS) is mandatory equipment for all vehicles since September 2007 by extension the government, although never indicating so in regulation, actually meant that all tires mounted to the car had to be compatible with the system. Thus the new "issue" to be resolved was how to protect the people foolish enough to want to put snow tires on their cars to improve handing during winter months. The answer was simple – don't allow installation of any wheels that were not equipped with the necessary TPMS sensors. That solution gave drivers the choice of not installing snow tires mounted on separate wheels, changing tires on wheel rims that had sensors (and run the risk of damaging the tires), or install sensors in the new wheels. Once again the value added to the owner (you can call that a private citizen) as compared to the cost of the answer was not addressed. But, the "issue" was resolved for now.

But wait, is the problem really solved or just waiting for the next engineering innovation that can be turned to an issue and mandated? Have you heard about "run flat" tires? How far away can that "issue" be? (Just as a note – cars equipped with "run-flat" tires are already required to have a TPMS installed).
As an aside, after writing this section, I took a road trip of about 3000 miles driving my car equipped with TPMS. On day three of the ten day trip the TPMS warning light on the dash and the message alert told me a tire had low pressure. Being a person who was trained to believe indicators, I promptly pulled over and mechanically took pressure readings on all of the tires. Imagine my confusion when none of the tires was out of specification. I later stopped at a service station and verified inflation in each tire. I completed the trip with a flashing indicator on the dash, proper pressure in the tires, and a "safety" system that was of no value to me. And to think, I learned to inspect my car at each gas stop and

to check tire pressure periodically. I guess that early training paid off. Imagine that.

By now you should understand that the concept of "issues" is really a general political construct. The real purpose of an issue discussion is to avoid the limiting role of government as defined by "We the people" and to gain support for actions that increase control by government and reduce the liberty and freedom of individuals. Knowing how to deal with issues without falling into the trap of Political Correctness or a perceived "common good" is essential for every conservative. The next several sections deal with prominent issues of the day and provide a more conservative viewpoint. The information presented for each issue cannot and should not be classed as "talking points" but should be analyzed as sound factual basis for discussion and debate.

A is for Abortion

No single political issue of the modern era has received greater attention or heightened emotions more than the issue called abortion or "a woman's right to choose". Coincidentally, no issue has so misused the English Language to foster emotional response as the issue of abortion.

This argument was being edited (2015) when the revelation that Planned Parenthood was manipulating abortions to enable the sale of fetal tissues to medical research facilities. That revelation certainly places in a different light the arguments made and supported by a primary abortion facilitator for the "right" to free and open abortion on demand.

There was a time (predating the push for "sex education" as a requirement to graduate from school) when the basic concepts of human biology were taught as a fact based course. One of the great secrets revealed in basic biology concerned the propagation of life and the process by which new humans (and other creatures) came into being. The course discussed those embarrassing things like males, females, the reproductive process, and the cycle of human bodies. The end result is that those who paid attention discovered that it took one male and one female to create new life through a process called impregnation. The ova carried by the female was fertilized by a spermatozoa provided by the male. While the specifics of how that actually happened may not have been discussed in detail, the end result of the process was pretty clear. One male, one female, one fetus. This relationship is critical in the understanding of the abortion (woman's right to choose) issue when addressing it from the conservative position.

In general, the liberal argument concerning abortion (woman's right to choose) is that a woman, who is pregnant, has the right to determine if she will or will not allow the pregnancy to go to completion. After all, it is her body that is being affected and the decision is one that she should be able to make with her doctor (perhaps) and without any outside interference. Please note that the decision process is what leads to the "woman's right to choose" label for the issue. In reaching her decision the woman has no need to consider impact on any other person or element, and is strongly supported by a rationale associated with rape, incest, and the health of the woman. This is the ultimate process of self-determination without regard to reasons for the pregnancy or any degree of personal responsibility. The strongest liberal argument is that of self-determination, and woe unto any who might even suggest that abortion on demand might be questionable.

Unfortunately, the argument presented by the liberal side and the condemnation of any opposition has resulted in a discussion in which morality and free choice are separated from fact and the element of character. Conservatives have commonly fallen into the trap of accepting the debate parameters set by the liberals only to discover that they are unable to carry forth any reasonable opposition. It is time to back away from the liberal playground and reassess the actual argument that can put the abortion issue into perspective and counter the liberal position.

Biologically the advent of pregnancy requires both a male and a female to actively participate. When pregnancy does occur, because it is the direct result of contribution of both participants, that result is the responsibility of both. In most cases, impregnation cannot occur if an effective barrier between the male sperm and the female egg is in place. Impregnation can also be prevented by various medical treatments specifically designed to prevent impregnation. In the event that some question may exist concerning the effectiveness of contraception processes or methods, there are available products to immediately terminate a potential unwanted pregnancy.

In the history of the world, only one possible conception of a fetus without the participation of both a man and a woman, has been alluded. Because that reported example is also the basis for a particular religious belief, most liberals would argue that it is a myth rather than reality. That said and accepted, the potential for "immaculate conception" in this day and age is eliminated.

Excluding rape, when a male and female engage in the activity that might result in pregnancy, they do so as a matter of choice. That choice includes an understanding of the potential consequences of the actions and a specific degree of personal responsibility and accountability for the actions taken. Excluding rape, when a male and a female engage in the activity that might result in pregnancy and do so without appropriate protective devices, they run the risk of transmitting and incurring sexually transmitted diseases and they do so as a matter of choice. That choice includes an understanding of the potential consequences of the actions and a specific degree of personal responsibility and accountability for the actions taken.

Termination of a pregnancy before natural birth is a potential natural function. In our current use of our language the natural early termination is called a miscarriage (meaning premature expulsion of a non-viable fetus from the uterus) and normally not an event anticipated or desired by either the female or male contributor. (Of note, the term "abortion", most common in use for this issue, applies to both natural and artificially induced terminations)

The termination of a pregnancy prior to full term as other than a natural act (effectively an artificially induced miscarriage) should be so labeled so that the discussion of the event can be better understood in both medical and lay terms. The terminology also more properly defines the act as a contrast to a natural miscarriage.

Maintaining a position that any action related to the continuation or termination of a pregnancy is the right of either participant ignores the joint nature of the condition. If a woman has some specific right to terminate an unwanted pregnancy why does not the male contributor have the same right?

When a pregnancy does occur without the specific active voluntary participation of the female or when for sound medical reason continuation of a pregnancy would endanger the life of the female (a condition that presumes no prior knowledge of the endangering conditions) induced miscarriage may be considered as an appropriate option to resolve the condition.

The basis of the rule of law is that all individuals are responsible for the actions that they willingly and actively engage in and the consequences thereof. It has been long held that ignorance of the law is no excuse and it follows that ignorance of potential consequences of an action is no excuse that would relieve the individual from accountability.

The moral objection to induced miscarriage as a matter of convenience is not sufficient reason to argue against that action. Presenting such an argument presumes that the female involved shares the same or similar moral standards as the person making the argument. Common sense would indicate that should that be the case the need for the argument would be moot. Forcibly imposing the moral standards of one person on another is not appropriate. Similarly, arguing that "life begins at conception" has no basis in law or American history. This is an important element in any argument because failure to adhere to fact compromises the effectiveness of the argument. The closest reference in the Constitution to status of people or citizens is found in the first sentence of Section 1. "All persons born or naturalized in the United States and subject to the jurisdiction thereof, are citizens of the United States and of the State wherein they reside."

Close examination of the facts and opinions related to induced miscarriage reveals a compelling argument that both avoids the emotional minefields sown by liberals and which challenges the average citizen to apply basic logic to their decision making process.

Conservatives should no longer refer to the act of artificially induced miscarriage as "abortion" but will use the correct terminology – artificially induced miscarriage. No doubt the liberals will attempt to continue to use their favorite term but conservatives need to correct the language to move the discussion and debate from emotion to fact.

Conservatives should not argue the exceptions for rape, incest, or properly founded health of the mother concerns. The arguments of the past were based on moral grounds and were not appropriate.

Conservatives should argue that "unwanted pregnancy" is the direct result of choices made by the active participants in the act leading to pregnancy. We will argue that in making the choices that they did the individuals had to understand the potential consequences and the additional risks that they incurred with regard to sexually transmitted diseases.

Conservative should argue that it is the norm for our society to hold individuals accountable for the consequences of their acts and not provide easy avenues of escape from accountability. Along those same lines, conservatives should argue that the actions and resultant consequences of individuals do not represent valid criteria for any other individual to support the ultimate choices made. Payment for birth control methods and artificially induced miscarriage are the responsibility of the individual and not society, as a whole.

Conservatives should argue that, contrary to the concept of the "woman's right to choose", the actions of the woman in question and the understanding that it requires both a male and a female to induce pregnancy, gives the male an equal right to choose.

The summation of the conservative argument is that unwanted pregnancy is the result of a poor decision making process by two people and the resolution of that condition should be a joint decision. In addition, the conservative argument should be that in all things, individuals must be held responsible and accountable for the actions that they take and the consequences of those actions.

If given the truth and compelling logic of the conservative argument, the general public continues to favor or support the irresponsible behavior associated with unwanted pregnancy and continues to condone uncontrolled artificially induced miscarriage, the problem faced has nothing to do with the "issue" of unwanted pregnancy but rather is a much deeper societal failure.

B is for "Bullying"

We are all aware of the ongoing effort to stamp out "bullying" in the lives of our children and in our society in general. Some have elevated the very thought of "bullying" to the crisis stage and have equated the bully to a person perpetrating life threatening physical and mental abuse on others.

Perhaps we should take a step back and put a bit of reality into the discussion. Yes, there are "bullies" out there who tend to impose their unkind and mean efforts to intimidate on others. There always have been and there always will be bullies. The standard definition of a bully is one who through physical size difference, aggressive behavior, or group association seeks to intimidate others and to control their acts and actions. We have all met bullies and, in some cases we have acted as bullies ourselves. Older children act out the age and size difference with their younger siblings at some point in their growing up. The more popular kids in school attempt to exercise some superior social position over the "nerds", the smaller kids, and the kids who are "different" in some manner. Social ostracism, assigning unflattering "names" and general harassment without physical abuse are most common. Unfortunately that type of behavior is part of growing up and cannot be eliminated.

When the activity becomes physical, results in damage to personal belongings, or extends to outright extortion, the bully steps over the line and needs to be corralled and disciplined. Tipping someone's books and papers to the ground or floor, breaking into a personal locker and damaging or taking personal items, or demanding payment to prevent direct personal abuse are not the actions of a bully but of a junior criminal in the making. Confusing simple name calling with extortion and lumping them together tends to minimize the significance of the more serious negative behavior. There is a vast difference between the level of negative interaction and that difference needs to be recognized in both the manner of intervention and the corrective action taken.

Is it OK to let kids call each other names? Probably not, but where do they get the role model for that behavior? Perhaps we should look at the manner in which adults, especially those involved in political discussion, relate to each other. For many adults, the first response to any disagreement with the position taken by another is to defame the character of that individual. Think about how often we use derogatory terms about those who do not support our personal ideas of what is right and wrong. It is almost unheard of for adults to have a political debate or discussion (or for two or more to discuss any issue with differing points of view) without at least one of the participants resorting to name calling or attributing the opponent with some derogatory motive. When was the last time there was a discussion of any substance when terms like "homophobic", "bigot", "racist", "woman hater" or similar did not enter the discussion? Yes, I know that is a major "weapon" in the progressive/liberal debate arsenal, but how is it different from the very thing those progressives and liberals are declaring a "crisis" for our children?

Adults have a responsibility to supervise their children and to make sure that the occurrence of bullying is minimized. They also have the responsibility to teach their kids to be tough and to prepare them for a world where bullying is a way of life for some. Bullying only works through effective intimidation. Therefore it is imperative to teach kids to not be intimidated and to center their actions and responses to others on earned self-worth and self-respect. Nothing hurts and stops a bully, young or old, faster and more completely than being laughed at.

C is for Crisis Management

You thought you had it all figured out and you knew exactly the "crisis" that posed the greatest threat to our way of life and well-being. Then along came another band of "scientists" or "experts" to tell us of a new and more dangerous threat. Now you are once again fully confused as to what we must do to protect yourselves and the rest of humanity.

Rachel Carson, in the 1960's, in her book "Silent Spring," predicted a full series of calamities from global starvation to the extinction of numerous species around the world. Of course, Carson named humans as the arch villains and set the stage for all of the doom and gloom prophesies to follow. Fortunately, not one of Carson's predictions has come true. None-the-less we continue down the trail she blazed.

Next, we, as a nation, assured ourselves that we would perish from the face of the earth if we did not take immediate steps to restore the cleanliness of our air and water to some pre-human intervention standard. The immediate targets were industries that were indeed polluting our water and air in the name of profit. However, that was a vestige of the entire industrial revolution, not only here but around the world. In short order (in a historical perspective) the significant pollution was brought to a halt and water and air quality restored. Unfortunately, having found a banner to march under, environmental activists continue to clamor for cleaner air and cleaner water, taking great liberty at "finding" conditions to fix. Our air and water supplies are cleaner today than at any time over the past 150 years but obviously that is not good enough.

Having found great success in "saving the planet" through their clean air/clean water causes, the "environmental scientific" community next set out to save from extermination any and all specie they considered "threatened" by humanity. The process was easy; identify a species as "threatened" or "endangered" under criteria created by the environmentalists and then empower the full force of government to curtail any action that might be considered detrimental to that species. The impact on individual people or local economies, through implementation of "protective measures," was not a significant consideration. The only thing that mattered was "saving the (fill in the blank)". The crusade became such a winner for the environmental forces that they were able to come up with new and unique ways to define "species" and thereby expand the "protective" net they wove about the country. Unfortunately, the number of "species" now being protected defies all reason and the impact on individuals is outrageous.

Several years ago, we were faced with the coming of a new "ice age". After all, the "science" of the time clearly showed a cooling trend in the earth's atmosphere and the final result was obvious. The entire northern half of the US would be buried under a thick sheet of glacial ice. The reasons for the cooling trends ran everywhere from devastation of the earth's rain forests to man created instability in the earth's oceans. The "ice age" was averted by the onset of "global warming".

According to environmental activists,the current trendy crisis is the destruction of our atmosphere by man-made greenhouse gasses, especially CO2. The specific culprit of this crisis is our use and dependence on fossil fuel. Of course America is the worst offender because we use more fossil fuel than any other nation and per capita figures really make the case for how terrible we are. Of course, the fact that the American economy has for many years, and still does, support the economies of the rest of the world is not a consideration. The fact that less than five percent of the nation's electrical power is generated by methods acceptable to the environmental radicals is not a consideration. Just because there is no reasonable alternative to fossil fuel available today or at any time in the foreseeable future is no reason to not immediately curtail the use of fossil fuel. The very fact that there is not one single scientific paper of repute that links human activity to global climate variation (not weather variations) does not phase the dedicated radicals in their effort to "save the earth". Of note, very few people in underdeveloped countries of the world care about the sources of the electrical power they so desperately want and need. Most would do most anything to have the standard of living enjoyed by the peoples of developed nations. Might that not also make it more probable that environmental concerns and positions are more closely aligned to those who already have a comfortable life and who can afford the luxury of the campaigns to save everything? If the environmentalists are successful in their efforts, who really will be the winners and the losers?

As this is being written, the State of California is in an apparent drought crisis. More correctly, the residents of Southern California and the Central Valley region are having a hard time satisfying all of the legislated and human related uses. There can be no doubt that California, and the entire US west coast, have experienced several years of lower than normal precipitation. The precipitation cycle for the area is a known occurrence. Most of the area affected relies on water from the mountains to their east and from major rivers fed by the melting mountain snow pack. The obvious answer to the problem is, knowing the precipitation cycle to exist, create larger reservoirs to hold water in anticipation of need and/or institute long term policies on water use that will sustain the continuing needs. Unfortunately, California has done neither. While they can find money to build a high-speed "bullet train" in the center of the state, money for improving the water system does not seem available. In addition, the State maintains a questionable environmental policy for a threatened species, allowing millions of acre feet of water to flow into the ocean rather than using that water to meet normal agricultural (growing food) or other human needs. The question is not "Is there enough water?" The real question is "Why should we not better preserve and use the water that is available to meet our needs?" That then drives the secondary question "Should protecting a single habitat for a specie take precedence over the real needs of humans?" Californians have to decide.

Over the past thirty or so years, and continuing today, we have lived in a world in which fear of ultimate destruction has been a mainstay

117

of the liberal, environmental left. Through their continued assault on man-kinds primary instinct for survival, they have tried to instill a condition of near constant fear for our lives and that of our loved ones and a never ending "call to action" to save the world.

The world was headed to certain overpopulation in which there would be no place for people to survive. Sorry, that did not happen.

The food production of the world would fail and we would all starve to death. Sorry, we produce more food each year. There is plenty of food to go around.

The supply of water for the world would be exhausted and we would all die of thirst. Still waiting.

There would be a collision of a massive comet and the earth, completely destroying our world. The docudramas have been good box office but poor science. (It is interesting that the same environmentalists that so opposed nuclear weapons embraced them to save the world.) The night sky remains clear.

A massive volcanic eruption at (pick your location) would envelop the earth in an ash cloud that would block the sun for years and we would all die. Another great movie theme.

A massive geologic occurrence along the (pick a name) fault line would either drop entire land sections into an ocean or split the world asunder. Of course the land movement would result in a colossal (1000 foot or larger) Tsunami that would complete the destruction. Several movies have tried to justify the "threat", but somehow we manage to survive. We should note that there was not much concern about "endangered species" when humans were number one on the hit list.

Of course we can't forget El Nino and La Nina, the scourge of the western ocean which were sure to destroy life as we knew it in America. They keep happening and so do we.

Now we are faced with "global warming", or is it "abrupt climate change"? We have trouble keeping them straight. The only apparent common factor between the two is that humans are responsible for whatever it is that is or is not going to happen. Somehow the continuing contributions of volcanoes, earthquakes, forest fires, natural global oceanic cycles, and natural global temperature cycles have now been discounted. Isn't science wonderful when it can sort out all of the bad things happening to our world and find that we are the bad guys? Should we wonder, did any of the "scientists" ever read "Silent Spring" and ponder the actual results? Equally interesting is the ability of the "real" scientists to pick and choose the "data" that validates their findings while blissfully ignoring the facts that effectively counter their arguments and point to different outcomes. Ours has become the age of computer models overriding actual observed information. We have made up our minds, don't confuse us with facts.

With all the contesting threats to our continued survival here on earth, we remain in a quandary about how we should prepare for our inevitable demise. It does seem that, no matter what we do to resolve one crisis, another pops up. All things considered, is it possible that simply turning our backs on the never ending crisis conspiracy and living our lives to the fullest would be most appropriate? Instead of spending our limited energies worrying about the fate of the world, perhaps it would be best to leave the worrying to those who wish to dedicate their lives to lost and worthless causes. As for me, (and Jimmy Buffett) "it's five o'clock somewhere".

D is for Death Penalty

There is good and evil in the world. There will always be a struggle between the two and without positive action by the forces of good, evil will prevail. There is no way to restrain or mitigate evil. Evil must be eliminated if good is to survive.

We live in a society of individuals where each of us has the duty and responsibility to protect not only our own rights but also those of all others. In order to do that, we, as a society, have established a set of operating parameters or laws and rules that we all agree to live by. While it is impossible to legislate either morality or individual behavior, it is possible to identify what behaviors are not acceptable to society and provide penalties for engaging in those behaviors. Every individual has the right to disregard the rules established by society and act in any manner they so desire. However, every individual who chooses to ignore the rules of society or act in a manner not acceptable to society must also be prepared to suffer the consequences of their actions. The society that establishes the parameters of performance also has the duty to hold those who violate the rules accountable. Without a system of rules and consequences, we would live in chaos and there would be no meaning to the concept of individual rights.

For every rule or restriction that society establishes, society must also set the price to be paid for violation of the rules. The rules must be simple and clear and the price to be paid for infraction must also be clearly identified. In this manner, the decision to violate a rule is a matter of personal choice and the individual making the choice is responsible for the consequences of the choice. No system could be more clear or more fair. Every individual knows the price of misbehavior before the fact and should take the price that society will extract into consideration before they make the decision to misbehave. Society always has the option to impose a lower cost for an infraction but that is the decision of society and not the violator.

There are some conducts that violate the rules of society which require a response that is both severe and appropriate. Taking the life of another person is the ultimate violation of that individual's rights. To do it knowingly and willfully is the ultimate evil. There can be no excuse for the premeditated termination of an innocent person's life or the taking of life in the act of some other violation of society's rules. Any person who participates in any act against society that results in the willful death of another must be prepared to pay whatever price society demands. It is the ultimate test of the principle of personal responsibility and the process of freedom of choice and consequences.

Many in our society believe that terminating the existence of an individual who has committed an act so heinous and contrary to the basic rules of society is an appropriate consequence. The act of the perpetrator was one of pure evil and it stands to reason that the response must be to eliminate that evil so that it may not occur again. The most correct response to ultimate evil is the ultimate consequence - the death penalty. Because society also applies a proven system of justice in the process to determine the guilt or innocence of any individual accused of a capital crime and because the burden of proof of the guilt of the individual is placed with society, a reasonable degree of protection is afforded the accused. Arguments that the system of justice is not absolute and not infallible have some merit but the ability of any accused person to demonstrate innocence after conviction belies those arguments. The position that we should allow all who are guilty to go free rather than execute an innocent person is nice rhetoric but has little to do with reality and ignores the existence of evil.

The system of justice established by society and placed in the hands of government serves to protect the innocent, bring the guilty to account, and to provide assurance to the victims that they have not suffered in vain. Far too often, in today's legal battles, the victims are forgotten or ignored as the legal representatives seek ways to use or subvert the intention of law in order to win their case. Society is not the winner when convictions are lost or overturned based on procedural error or a simple error of omission by an individual in the process. It is those kinds of cases that provide the "facts" for those opposed to maximum punishment as they argue based on cases reversed on appeal. Of course those arguments do not identify which cases were procedural errors and not the actual guilt of the accused. Nor do those arguments identify how the actions in another unrelated case directly affect the outcome of a specific death penalty case.

The checks and balances of the judicial system, as well as the social conscience of the community, are suitable and effective arbiters in the determination of application of the death penalty. The death penalty can only be sought when the violation committed is one for which the penalty has been authorized. Even then, the prosecution process must make a positive determination that the death penalty will be sought before the actual matter goes to trial. The court of law, the selected jurors, the prosecution (government acting for society), and the defense (acting for the accused) are all aware that the death penalty is a possible outcome if the accused is found guilty of the charges. Even in the event of a conviction, there is a pre-sentence hearing at which additional testimony is allowed to attempt to mitigate the conduct of the convicted and seek a sentence other than death. The appeals process for any death sentence is lengthy and complete. We are a far cry from the days of holding court in the saloon, finding the bad guy guilty, and hanging him the same afternoon.

There is always a loud argument (long on volume, short on logic) that the same people who support the death penalty oppose abortion and that is hypocritical. Nothing could be further from the truth. The death penalty is only imposed on individuals who knowingly and willfully made a choice to take the life of another or to commit a crime against society of similar extent. The victim had no choice in the outcome of the acts committed by the perpetrator. The purpose of the death penalty is understood to permanently remove a person of evil from society. The convicted individual is being held responsible for the consequences of the choices he made. Abortion (discussed in another chapter) is a choice made by an individual to terminate a life (or potential life) in response to the consequences of an earlier choice. The individual who elects to undergo abortion is specifically evading the consequences of a previous choice and is ignoring the demands of personal responsibility. In the case of abortion the victim (embryo or fetus, your choice) ,and has no voice in the decision to abort.

E is For Economic Development

Economic development is the direct result of good or bad choices by individuals and the reaction of governments and other people to those choices. Like all things in life, economic development is a matter of choice.

To properly set the stage for a discussion about the relative political importance of economic development we must first understand the basic political interests of both sides. Conservatives favor a robust, strong and growing economy because of the opportunity presented to individuals to improve their personal lives, to enjoy freedom, and to exercise liberty. A strong and growing economy provides choice and allows for growth in personal well-being. Progressives, on the other hand, favor a slow or minimal growth in the economy. They need the continued lack of choice and opportunity to increase personal dependency on government to meet minimal life demands. Progressives use a controlled economy to move more and more people away from personal self-dependence and onto total dependence on government programs. While Conservatives tend to get tied up in numbers relating to historic growth comparisons and rates of growth, the only numbers Progressives care about is how many more people have been forced into government support programs. With that clarity in mind we are better prepared to both understand and argue the issue of economic development.

The oft repeated wisdom that "you have to spend money to make money" is at the very core of economic development. An individual or group of individuals acting together for common purpose choose to use their assets to complete an effort that will provide goods or services to the public. The people who put forth the assets are called "investors", and they are taking a risk that their investment will, in fact, result in a reasonable financial return on that investment. Investors are the ones who make possible the development of ideas into viable marketable products that we use every day. Investors are responsible for starting the stores and markets that offer the goods and services we use in our lives.

Investors are the ones who bring us "the good life" that we all enjoy, provide employment opportunities, and allow us the potential to become part of the "investor" clan ourselves.

It bears repeating that investors use assets that they have earned or gained through the fruits of their labors or those of their associates. Investors or entrepreneurs place those assets at risk when they make a choice of where to invest. There is no guarantee that an investment will be successful and many are not. There is no guarantee that the assets risked will be recovered or that the investors will be able to walk away from failure without additional liability beyond the original asset investment. It is the opportunity to gain a return on those investments that make the investors take the risk. In modern conversation, the "return on investment" has been replaced incorrectly by the term "profit" and investors are linked together as "rich opportunists." It should be clear, with a basic understanding of economic development, nothing could be further from the truth.

There can be no doubt that some investors "strike it rich" and the return on investment is enormous. That return, however, is directly related to the desirability of the product or service to the public and the willingness of the public to trade their assets for the product or service. Bill Gates is not one of the richest men in the world because he routinely "rips off" or "fleeces" the public with an inferior product that adds little or nothing to our personal value. Whether you like the Microsoft product line or not, there can be no doubt as to the positive impact of Microsoft products on the world economy and our personal lives. For other investments, that the initial investments were made and the companies founded and prospered, has provided an opportunity for many of us to become investors on our own. Our individual retirement funds or personal investment funds are made with the same return on investment concept as considered by major investors. We are also looking for return on our investment. In that light, it becomes just a bit confusing when individuals who are invested in stocks or bonds take exception to others who enjoy the benefits of similar investments. It is really hard trying to understand how "Wall Street" can be bad when my stock portfolio is growing at a healthy rate.

Please note that individual investors, that means people just like you and me, are the ones responsible for economic growth and development in our American economic system. Also note the relationship between personally held assets and the concepts of investment. This is a key relationship because it helps to better understand the role that government plays in economic development.

Government does not have a source of assets other than those they acquire from citizens through taxation or fees. Because government does not have the power to earn "assets", government does not have the power to invest in anything. Government is limited to completing the duties and responsibilities we have delegated to government. Government is limited in its ability to tax only to the level necessary to complete those assigned responsibilities. Therefore, it should be obvious, when a politician or appointed bureaucrat tells us that "government is making an investment" they are lying through their teeth. Building roads, bridges, tunnels, and ferry systems is not an "investment in our future". It is a completion of basic delegated responsibilities. Conversely, enacting laws and regulations that either limit unnecessarily the opportunity for private investment and economic growth or imposition of taxes and fees that have the effect of restricting such growth, is a feature of negative economic development often exercised by government. In short, government cannot create positive economic development because it does not have the asset base for the essential investment. Government is not empowered to invest in anything. Government can support economic development by the faithful execution of its assigned responsibilities. Unfortunately. Government far too often hinders or restricts economic development through regulatory control that is of little or no benefit to anyone other than the government bureaucrats who enforce the rules.

The lesson of economic development then boils down to a couple of basic principles.

Economic development is the direct result of the willingness of individuals to invest their personal assets with the anticipation of a reasonable return on that investment.

Economic development provides the opportunity for all to find gainful employment and earn assets of their own which they may later invest with the anticipation of reasonable return.

Investors who risk their personal assets for economic development earn the returns they gain through their investment. They also face the potential of failure and total loss. Because there is no guarantee of success, any success that results is a rightful gain to the investors.

Government does not have the ability to invest in anything. By proper execution of its responsibilities, government can support continued economic development. By exceeding its authorities, government can only restrict, hinder, and retard economic development.

One of the primary arguments offered that the "rich are greedy and only want to take advantage of people" has little or no merit in fact. Investors create companies that provide jobs for everyone else. They provide goods and services to the public that individuals want and at prices that individuals are willing to pay. The complete product equation is, in fact, set by the public and the price they are willing to pay for a product or service. To bring the product to market, the investor (or his company) needs to consider the cost of goods sold, the cost to bring to market, and, unfortunately, the government's share of the product cost. Cost of goods sold is simply the total cost of raw materials, labor, production cost, and overhead cost to prepare the product for market. Only some of those elements are actually costs under the control of the investor. Cost to bring to market includes things like transportation, storage, and the price the middle man and retailer are willing to pay to put the item on the shelf. Finally the government gets its bite most frequently at several points along the path from raw materials to sold product. The investor has no control over the government take. At the end of the line, the final price to the public has to be one that covers all the costs and still provides a return for the investor. It should be easy to see that an increase in any of the elements that are involved in the cost of bringing the product to market must be reflected in an increase in the end product. It will be important to remember that relationship when we deal with the issue of government established minimum pay for workers or the impact of labor agreements on prices.

F is for "Free Lunch" Lifestyle (Entitlements)

There was a time in our American history when the personal attribute and characteristic of self–dependence was the norm for all individuals. It was a part of being American and gave rise, in part, to the idea of the American Dream. It was the driving force behind those who came to America to find a new life and better circumstances for themselves and their children. Even those newly arrived in America or those who existed at the low end of the economic strata found a way to provide the basics for themselves and to preserve the dignity associated with self-dependence. That essential conservative characteristic has been forfeited by far too many Americans. In too many instances the characteristic of self-dependence has been forsaken by the lure and easy times of "entitlements".

The federal government, in an effort to "fix" a perceived problem with "poverty" in some limited part of the population, created a much larger problem.   A progressive program to provide for the most poor of Americans may have started with good intentions but has grown into an economic disaster. We are now faced with the actual problem of a nation with about half of its people on some sort of government support program, about half of its people not paying the taxes that run the country, and all or most of those individuals qualified as voters able to vote to continue or extend the programs from which they now benefit.

In the understanding of government programs, let us be very clear about the difference between "earned benefit" and entitlement. Earned benefits include such things as pensions that were earned through work for the government or a government entity. Social Security and Medicare payments to those who actually paid into the system are earned benefits. The interest earned on federal or other jurisdiction government bonds is an earned benefit from the investment made. Veterans Disability payments and services to veterans are earned benefits in return for the service provided. The common denominator is that all of the earned benefits are the direct result of a contract of one form or another between government and the individual who earned the benefit. The individual performed as required by contract and the government is now completing their contractual obligation.

The concept of "entitlement" grows directly from some government legislative action that creates a support program for individuals. When the federal government created the Food Stamp Program (now the Supplemental Nutrition Assistance Program or SNAP) the intent was to make sure that the people with very low or no income had basic subsistence food to eat. Though well intentioned, the program was not well administered, the criteria for benefits were widened, and the number of individuals receiving support grew continuously. Today some 46 million people (about 13 percent of the American population) receive "benefits" under the program. Many have been provided for under the Food Stamp Program for so long (in some case into the third or fourth generation) that the benefit has become the standard and the individuals now consider themselves "entitled" to the support. The down side of the program, other than the ever growing and non-sustainable cost, is that the dependence on the food stamp program has removed incentive for personal effort to grow and escape from the system. In fact, in some cases, the criteria for continued program enrollment make the decision to accept work a difficult decision for the individual. Accepting a paying job might result in sufficient earning to lose eligibility under the program and still be unable to afford basic subsistence. The program has become such a pervasive part of low income America that the federal government actually recruits new people to enter the program and receive benefits. The need for development of personal self-dependence is destroyed by this kind of program.

Medicaid is another example of a well-intentioned idea gone wrong. The original intent was that, with some government support, low income individuals or families would be eligible for limited health care. The primary targets were pregnant women and young children. Seemed like a good idea at the time. Unfortunately the unexpected consequences of combining a federal social medicine program with both state regulation and self–imposed performance criteria by medical professionals soon brought chaos and growth to the program.

The Medicaid system failed to recognize the importance of or provide appropriate support for continuance of the "family doctor" approach to medicine. The rules and regulations controlling eligibility, levels of service, and payment, were coupled with mountains of paperwork for care providers. It became impractical for a single doctor or a small office with several doctors to accept or rely on Medicaid patients for their business (Yes, medical care is a business). In a double edged sword of unintended consequences, since private practitioners could not reasonably handle Medicaid users, the only alternative was for the patients to rely on larger medical facilities. Unfortunately, those facilities did not have large staffs of "family practice" doctors and the answer became to use the Emergency Room as the entry point for medical care. Because the medical profession has a self–imposed standard of not refusing medical care to any in need, there was no way to turn away those who could not pay or the Medicaid patients. In short order, hospital Emergency Rooms began to look like what was previously a simple doctor's waiting room and the demands on medical and administrative staff grew.   The end result of this entire out of control "entitlement" has been a steady rise in the cost of medical treatment for all and a continuing unnecessary overload of our health care system.

It has become common place in America for a serving President or a candidate for high office to "decree" some new entitlement for the people. Here are some examples. Every individual must be eligible to attend college for free. . Every individual must have a cell phone for basic communications. Every American is entitled to a living wage as mandated by government. Leave from work to address "family emergencies" must be paid leave available to all. Mass transit must be available to all Americans so they can get to work. There are many more. They all have the common denominator of being "free", with government picking up the tab. How government gets that money (can you say increased taxes or borrow?) does not appear to be a concern. The "what's in it for me generation" has apparently grown into the "I deserve everything I want for free" generation. It is past time to put an end to the foolishness.

Perhaps even more damaging than the "entitlements" that individuals believe that they have a "right" to, are the entitlements that our elected representatives have created for themselves. Elected representative at all levels of government enjoy "perks" that range from free parking, low cost barber shops, low cost dining rooms, and well-furnished office spaces in several locations to taxpayer funded junkets on "fact-finding missions" throughout the world and extensive multi-media communications services to "keep their constituents informed". They also include extremely generous medical care and retirement benefits. The use of the infamous "earmarks", which supposedly are to make sure that essential projects in their home districts are properly funded, are little more than self-approved "entitlements" to buy votes. Our representatives are paid a salary or some level of compensation to perform the responsibilities of the office to which they sought election. Beyond that, the only thing they should be entitled to is simple office space, a minimal staff, nominal office materials support, routine communications support, and a place to sit in the house or senate chamber. Anything else they want they should have to provide for themselves just like the rest of us do. Any retirement program for elected representatives should mirror that of the appropriate civil service employees. Health care should be nominal and part of a participating program. In short, getting elected should not be an open route to the treasury for personal enrichment or aggrandizement. Limiting the "entitlements" enjoyed by elected officials and representatives should be a primary objective for Conservatives.

G is for "Gay" Rights

On the day that the doctor in a hospital delivery room announces "Congratulation Ms. Smith, you have a healthy, bouncing baby transgender" I will reconsider my outlook on this issue. Until then, I will let physiology and moral character guide my judgement. That said, I will acknowledge that while science has not been able to identify a physical explanation for homosexual behavior, a possibility of psychological abnormality does exist. If it is a mental abnormality, why would we treat it any different than any other similar problem?

In order to place this discussion in context, it is appropriate to understand the statistical significance of homosexual behavior. Numerous statistical studies have identified a continuing 1.5 to 1.7% of our American population as describing their sexual orientation as homosexual (male and female combined). As an interesting comparison, when the general population is asked about the number of homosexuals in America, they assume the number to be in the range of 20% or higher. Obviously the "media exposure", on the part of the homosexual community, has had a significant impact on the discussion when it comes to understanding real numbers.

The ascendency and success of the "Gay Marriage: and "Gay rights" movement is also one of the most prominent examples of national bullying in recent history. The LGBT community portrayed itself as victims of the "straights" who treated then with hate and disrespect for what they were and not who they were. Without a shred of evidence other than individual anecdotal stories, isolated instances of conflict, and a direct disregard of established moral standards of the overwhelming majority, the LGBT community executed a program of labeling any who were not in direct and clear support of their lifestyle as homophobic, ant-gay, moralistic prudes, and hate mongers. The LGBT movement was able to silence opposition by false accusation and character assassination. Should there be any wonder why so many now have deeper resentment and lack of respect for the community as a whole?

There is an ongoing effort to instill in society a belief that an individual making a choice (or subject to an undefined psychological abnormality) toward sexual preference have "rights" equal or superior to others in society and by that choice that individual is part of a minority and deserves special "protection". The argument has no identified basis. That it is furthered and "supported" by declarations of "opinion presented as "fact" and "evidence" based in non-validated "science" certainly does not substantiate either the argument or the outcome it demands.

Before moving into the full discussion of the "rights" associated with homosexual activity, it is significant to identify the language to be used. Of note, honest discussion of this and any other subject can be conducted only when common definition and common language is applied to assumption and argument used in the discussion. The condition commonly referred to as "Gay", covering a wide range of sexual choices, is a slang substitute for homosexual. The actual meanings of sexual terms are as follows:

Male: Of, relating to, or designation of the sex that has the organs to produce spermatozoa for fertilizing ova.

Female: Of, relating to, or designation of the sex that produces ova or bears young.

Homosexual: Relating to, typical of, or displaying homosexuality.

Homosexuality: Sexual desire for others of one's own sex. Sexual activity with another member of the same sex.

Lesbian: A woman whose sexual orientation is to women

Bi-sexual: Of or relating to both sexes.. Having both male and female reproductive organs; hermaphroditic. Of, relating to, or having a sexual orientation to persons of either sex.

Gender: The condition of being female or male; sex. Females or males considered as a group.

Transvestite; A person who dresses and acts in a style or manner traditionally associated with the opposite sex.

Gay: Showing or marked by exuberance or happy excitement. Bright, especially in color. Full of, or given to, social pleasures. Dissolute. Homosexual.

It is absolutely clear that sexual definition is a condition of birth and is defined by the physical characters inherent to the fetus and then the child. Determination of sex as either male or female is not a matter of choice. To openly deviate from the condition of physiology of birth is a matter of choice (or perhaps mental deviation). Only through the corruption of language to include the term "gay" to substitute for homosexual does the discussion of homosexual behavior become acceptable in normal society. However, changing the language to confuse the argument does not change the underlying choice of behavior or the foundations of societal norms.

Well over 75 percent of Americans identify affiliation with a religion that does not accept homosexual activity as either normal or morally correct. While religion should not be the sole basis for opinion concerning the behavior of others, there is no way to reasonably exclude those moral beliefs. For an individual to take a stand on moral religious beliefs is, in fact, a protected right guaranteed by our Constitution. While those generally held moral positions may not be mandates on behavior of others they do constitute a sound basis for acceptance and toleration of behaviors. If that were not the case, where would any social restriction of behavior have a basis?

Marriage is a creation of the church (or a religious group) to recognize a bond between a man and a woman in a union that is intended to last for a life time and serve as the basis for procreation and the continuance of a society. Because marriage is the creation of a religion (not the state) and because religions are supposed to be the earthly representations of our creator, it may be argued that marriage is a right endowed upon us by the Creator. That is the only manner in which marriage may be considered as, or addressed as, a "right". It also follows that since the religions addressing marriage identify it as a union between a man and a woman, extension of the sacrament of marriage to any other combination but those should not be possible. The state may control the authority to issue a license to homosexuals to "marry" but the government may not mandate that any religion or church must perform or honor homosexual marriage.

Argue as you might, because of the underlying nature of marriage, applying that sacrament to any other than a man and a woman is not possible. If society determines that it is in its own best interest to create law and regulation concerning privilege or responsibility associated with the marriage of a man and a woman, that certainly is a function of society so long as the unalienable rights of the individuals are not limited or restrained in any way.

If society desires to recognize and even formalize the union of a homosexual couple, society may do so. That union, regardless of what society may call it, is not a marriage in the true form of a marriage and to make argument that it is defies logic.

The 2015 decision by the US Supreme Court that would extend the right of marriage to gay couples as a constitutionally protected "civil right" marks another great overstep by that court and a clear disregard for the Constitution. Finding support for their decision in the Fourteenth Amendment has the same validity as finding an "art masterpiece" in a garage sale. The wording of the Amendment referenced by the court reads "No State shall make or enforce any law which shall abridge the privileges or immunities of citizens of the United States; nor shall any State deprive any person of life, liberty, or property without the process of law, nor deny to any person within its jurisdiction the equal protection of the law." That the Fourteenth Amendment was adopted specifically to address the recognition and legal status of those previously held in slavery did not seem to influence the Court. Of course they have used the most liberal interpretation of that Amendment to extend federal power in other instances. The Court also failed to recognize the authority delegation of the Tenth Amendment and took from the individual states a responsibility and authority that more properly belongs to the states. Finally, the very nature of the ruling by the Court destroys the concept of marriage and opens the door to any and all combinations of individuals who might seek marriage to include polygamy, incest based marriage, and other combinations. Equally important, by finding Gay marriage as a protected "right", the Court has placed a significant burden on any business persons or clergy who do not support "Gay" marriage, on moral grounds, to carry the burden of proof of their position under law. In essence the Court has denied a clear and fully protected right to freedom of religious and moral belief, in favor of a created "right" to gay marriage. Of note, since the decision by the Supreme Court, Gay Rights activist groups in my local area have renamed themselves LBTGQ with the Q standing for "Queer". I anticipate that anyone outside that small protected community that uses the term "queer" to define either a person or the community will be subject to condemnation for "hate speech" and possible legal action.

A decision to support or recognize contractual unions of individuals outside the traditional and clear concept of marriage belongs to society as a whole and not to government. The decision to grant or recognize a union of a homosexual couple is not a matter of "civil rights" in that it is based entirely on individual choice and not a matter beyond the control of the individuals.

H is for Home Ownership

One of the specific reasons that the citizens of England who resided in the American colonies rebelled against the British government was the issue of home ownership and the rights associated with that ownership. Specifically, colonists did not wish to have the Crown dictate that private home owners would be required to house British troops in those homes.

Today there are various aspects of home ownership that are of interest. In each instance, it is understood that ownership of a home (private property) is gained by virtue of the results of personal effort and the fruits of individual labor. There is no "right" to home ownership because it is a privilege earned by the individual. There are very specific rights associated with ownership of a home or property but not the actual ownership itself. The rights associated with ownership and private property will be addressed in a separate chapter.

An individual earns home ownership through various legal means (purchase, homestead, estate gain, gift, or similar). The ownership is documented legally and becomes a part of the records of the state. The most common means of gaining home ownership is through purchase. In that transaction the individual exchanges the wealth gained through personal effort for the property in question. The wealth may be already earned or an obligation against future gains. The transfer price is agreed upon by the current owner of the property and the individual purchasing the property. In a straight cash or equal barter transaction the sale is straight- forward and simple. That all changes when a third party becomes involved and a loan against future earnings is used for the purchase. This is also the point where the concept of a right to home ownership fails.

A third party offering to invest their funds by loaning them to an individual has every right (cash is private property) to establish criteria for that loan. Historically, the lender has required a good faith financial involvement by the purchaser in the form of an equity position (down payment) in the property. For a number of years the expected equity was about 20 percent of the purchase price of the home. The lender also required a reasonable degree of assurance that the individual asking for the loan had a solid work history and would be able to repay the loan as contracted. The final determination regarding the issue of the loan rests with the lender.

In the recent past, government has become more involved in the arena of home ownership and the means and methods of offering loans to potential purchasers. Government regulations, over time, have tended to concentrate on new construction homes under a system of central planning. The result has been the reduction of homes on the market and the cost of individual homes. The reasons for those results are beyond this discussion but are well documented. Homes became more difficult to purchase and the prices went up. In response, government instituted programs that provided "insurance" for lenders so that they could increase risk associated with loans. At first the risk was associated with smaller equity positions by the purchaser. Later the risk was extended to not require proof positive of the economic well-being of the individual or demonstrated reliability in the means to repay the loan. The end result was inevitable. The government created a false social environment that touted home ownership as a universal right for all. Government established the policies and rules that both allowed and encouraged individuals who had no economic ability to support home ownership to purchase homes. When the bubble finally broke, as it had to, all home owners were hurt by a massive market decline and those without the ability to continue loan payments suffered foreclosure and loss of their homes. Even at that point, government tried to intervene to extend the myth that they had created. The real outcome of the entire mess was a clear understanding that if you do not have the economic ability to place an equity position in a home and repay the loan associated with the purchase, you should not be a home owner. Unfortunately, the lessons of the recent past have not resonated in the halls of government. Today, so soon after the housing and mortgage collapse, and while the economy is still trying to recover, the federal government is back at it with programs and regulations that would draw those not able to actually afford home ownership back into the market place. The government actually penalizes banks and lending institutions that do not make funds (called private money) available to the most risky of borrowers. Continuation of these policies will certainly fiscally ruin both the borrowers, and those who have funds invested with the borrowers. For some unknown reason, our government representatives do not understand that homeownership is not a universal privilege and that personal fiscal responsibility must be a part of the homeownership decision.

Once you have made the decision (choice) to become a home owner you incur several obligations to yourself and others. A home is normally the single largest personal investment for most people. It represents the accumulation of their wealth over time as their equity position in the home increases. The home owner has a personal obligation to themselves and their family, if appropriate, to use and maintain the property in a manner so as to retain its value. The home owner has an obligation to neighbors and community to use and maintain the house in a manner so as to reflect the values of the community and to not impose on the wellbeing of others. Finally, because homes are a primary source of tax revenue for all governments at the state and local level, the owner has an obligation to pay those taxes in a proper manner. Because conservatives have a fine sense of personal responsibility, carrying out the obligations of a home owner should be a natural extension of that ownership.

I is for Immigration

It is frequently said that America is a nation of immigrants. That is absolutely true but it is not the full story. America is also a melting pot that takes "the poor, the tired, and the hungry" from around the world and assimilates them into the most unique and powerful people in the world. America, like no other nation in the world, is the final destination for many who wander in search of a home and a place to belong.

The argument that once a nation of immigrants, without apparent restriction, we should continue on that path today. While there is some validity to the factual basis for the argument, that position fails to recognize that for more than 100 years our nation has controlled immigration with law, regulation, and procedure. It is the open violation of those laws that presents the problems we face today. Those individuals who seek to come to America, as visitors or residents, are subject to our laws for entry into the country and then the laws of the nation so long as they remain here. For a non-citizen to expect any different or for our nation to operate contrary to that basic understanding is not in the best interest of America or the individuals concerned.

With all of those things being true it is also critical to understand that America, and no single state of the United States, can reasonably expect to accept and provide for every person who wishes to come to America. Like every other nation on earth, the United States has a system of immigration that allows a certain number of individuals to enter the country each year. Under normal conditions, a person entering the country needs to be sponsored by someone already here to ensure that the new arrival is properly cared for and supported in their various needs. Those arriving legally are provided appropriate documentation that will allow them to find and accept work, attend school, and live within our communities. There are a wide variety of permissive documentations but the common factor is that the holder has the permission of the United States to enter into and remain within the country for a certain period of time. The immigrant, in return for the right to be in America, agrees to abide by our laws, be self-reliant, pay taxes and fees as may be appropriate, and leave the country at a specific time if that is stipulated in the entry agreement. Under this system, the United States takes specific caution to not allow persons with criminal records, serious illnesses, no visible means of support, or demonstrated views or actions contrary to the best interest of America from entering the country. The legal immigration system has been in place for a significant period of time and serves well both America and those who desire to immigrate

There is also a separate category of immigrants who are properly attempting to flee repression in their home country. The United States offers "refugee" status to people from around the world who would otherwise be in danger from the action of the governments of their home nations. The requirements for establishing refugee status are clear, and while a temporary status may be established, the final decision about the ability of the individual to remain is subject to a detailed legal process. It is not enough to claim "refugee" status, the fact of the threat to the individual must be demonstrated with the burden of proof being placed on that individual. As a general rule, any individual arriving in the United States seeking refugee status or political asylum is given the benefit of the doubt for initial entry and provided for until such time as the actual status is determined. Seldom is anyone who reaches our shores with a reasonable claim for refugee status rejected or turned away.

With the provisions of the legal immigration system clearly established and working, it is apparent that those who enter the United States, not in compliance with the legal entry systems in place, have done so illegally and violated US law. It should also be evident that, in order to sustain proper functioning of the legal immigration system, the US must exercise close control over its borders and entry points to the country. Without that effective control, the provisions of the legal immigration system become ineffective and meaningless.

Individuals who enter the United States without the prior permission and approval of the United States are illegal aliens. No "wordsmithing" or "political correctness" can change that fact. The first duty of the federal government with respect to illegal aliens is to bring them into custody and immediately deport them to their country of origin. The US must also adopt policies that prevent the creation of a natural citizen when a pregnant woman illegally enters the country simply to use the medical facilities available or to create citizenship for the newborn. Without such a policy, we are rewarding illegal behavior with a status that can later be used to circumvent the intent of other laws.

Unfortunately, because the federal government has failed to properly exercise its responsibilities with respect to illegal immigration, the country now has a very large number of illegal aliens living among us and enjoying all but a few of the rights of American citizens or legal immigrants. We have never been able to successfully debate a solution to the problem because the conservative side wants to base an argument of fact while the progressive side forwards an emotion based position. There is, however, an answer.

1. Establish a date specific by which every person in the US, not a citizen or a holder of legal immigration documents, must declare themselves to the government. Each of those individuals would be fully documented and placed in a tracking program.

2. Of that number, any who have been resident continuously in the US for at least 7 years (on a date specific) and who are gainfully employed (or part of a self-supporting family), who have paid all appropriate taxes and fees and who have no record of criminal activity, will be issued a unique temporary worker card that will allow them to remain and continue in their job. They will be expected to complete and file the appropriate request for immigration documentation. All conditions of this provision depend on positive

documentation and supporting evidence provided by the individual.

3. Any person who has illegally entered the United States and who has not been in the country for at least 7 years continuously shall be deported. Status of employment and of payment of taxes are not a consideration. The individual shall be allowed to take all accumulated private property with them, including all personal funds (regardless of amount). Any property not being taken may be sold on the open market with the revenues accruing to the individual. The individuals shall pay all costs associated with removal of private property from the US.

4. Any person who is the legal parent of a child born in the US but who is not in the country legally, shall be offered the option of meeting the employment and self-supporting status (see #2 above) or being deported. The child may be left behind in the care of legal citizens of the US or taken with the parents. If deportation is the option elected, the parents and the child may petition for accelerated consideration for legal immigration.

5. Any individual who has a criminal record or who has committed criminal acts and is in the country illegally shall be deported without further processing.

6. People who are apprehended as illegal aliens shall not be released on their own recognizance with a promise of appearance at a later court or hearing date. They shall become the immediate wards of the state and shall be held for appropriate action. The process for determining the immigration status of persons held shall be prompt and simple. If illegal entry is determined, immediate deportation shall follow. The individual being considered for determination shall have appropriate legal counsel but the process shall be limited to immigration status with the burden of proof on the individual. An individual filing an appeal to the determination shall be allowed to do so while in the country of origin through appointed counsel in the US.

7. Any individual who is determined to have entered the US illegally on 2 or more occasions and who has been previously deported shall be permanently denied legal entry into the US.

8. States shall not issue drivers licenses or similar identification cards to individuals without proof of citizenship or legal residence in the US. Driver's licenses that are issued to legal residents who are not citizens shall be uniquely marked to indicate that status. A driver's license shall not be considered valid proof of US citizenship unless the license specifically includes that information. A driver's license that does not specifically identify the holder as a citizen of the US shall not be accepted as proof of citizen ship for purpose of voter registration or travel outside of or return to the Unites States from abroad.

9. Employers found to have knowingly (includes not properly executing employee eligibility provisions) employing illegal aliens shall be fined to the full extent of the law.

10. Police officers of all jurisdictions will have the authority to verify the resident status of any individual who is otherwise subject to a legal stop for a violation of the law. These verifications will not be considered as "profiling". When an illegal alien is apprehended, that individual will be held and turned over to federal authorities for processing as quickly as possible. The federal authorities must accept individuals so apprehended without delay and with full intent of proper processing.

150

J is for Jihad and The War on Terror

In several other locations in this book there are discussions about foreign policy and Military Service. Those discussions are generally limited to what we consider normal conditions in the world. Unfortunately, in today's world we face a major new force; that of terrorism not associated or directly linked to any specific state or nation. This is the international war brought to us by those forces dedicated to terror as a way to gain power and control over some portion of the world or by those who seek eventual world domination. Unfortunately, there are also some nations that find it in their best interest to spread unrest in the world and serve as the state sponsors of terrorism. Those nations do not engage themselves directly in terrorist acts but do provide the support necessary for their surrogates to wage a war of terrorism.

Regardless of the declared basis for a terror action, be it religious or secular, the response to that action must be positive and resolute. In the case of a nation that conducts terrorist activities, the answer is generally clear; a declaration of war against that nation and the conduct of hostilities until resolution is achieved. In the instance of terrorist activities not associated with a nation the response in action must be similar but the process for completing the response action is not quite so clear.

First and foremost, it is essential that, in addressing terrorism, we properly identify the activities as those of war, declared or undeclared, and that the terrorist as combatants and not simple criminals. It is important to note that in almost every case, the terrorists "declare war" on some nation, groups of nations, religious affiliations, or social assemblies. That the terrorists are not a recognized nation does not deter them from taking on the trapping of a state to provide a cover of legitimacy to their actions. None-the-less, terror groups are not nations and do not deserve the considerations extended to nations when war is declared.

In almost every instance (I could not identify a variant case but I will make allowance for that possibility), the sole purpose of a terrorist action is to subjugate and dominate some specific group. There is no apparent goal of acquiring and holding territory other than that which might be associated with the ultimate goal of subjugation. The example of the declared "Caliphate" by Islamic State terror groups is not one of holding ground but one of subjugating people. The desired outcome is always the termination of the power of one group and the total power of the terror group. There is no room or practical way for any other negotiated resolution.

The only acceptable end to a terrorist activity is the complete and final destruction of both the active terrorists and the underlying support system that allows them to exist and operate. In short, that means carrying the military action to the terrorists and to any state or nation that provides support or succor to terrorists. The termination of individuals (yes, that means death) and the complete degradation of the ability of a state to continue to wage or support terrorist activities is essential. Anything less is a waste of time. The elimination of terrorist activity is a long term commitment. Terrorists have proven time and again that they are willing to wait for success. Terror organizations are most adept at maintaining a level of activity that achieves limited goals while waiting for the opposition to tire and quit. The only effective way to counter that reality is to accept the timeline set by the terrorist and to pursue every possible opportunity to carry the fight to them.

Fighting terrorism is not a matter of the decisions by one political party or another or one nation or another. Terrorism is a continuing threat to world peace and stability. Terrorism can only be defeated fully when all of the nations of the world join together to end the threat. Unfortunately, the very international organization created to counter threats to world peace, the United Nations, appears to be more interested in addressing human rights in non-terror nations and the social impacts of the weather than addressing its primary function. As a result, individual nations must join together to counter and eliminate the threat.

In 1983 America was faced with the first real terror action against the nation; the bombing of the Marine barracks in Beirut. In the intervening years from the barracks bombing until 2001, there were numerous other terrorist incidents that targeted the US. Unfortunately Americans failed to respond with sufficient force and the terrorists grew more bold. This all came to an immediate end on September 11, 2001 when terrorist activity was brought home to America. The terror action of 9/11 could not be ignored or met with cruise missile strikes in the desert. Terror came to America and it is here to stay until such time as America decides to take the actions necessary to eliminate the threat from the world. There really is no other choice.

Politicians have tried to find a way around or through the commitment that is necessary to counter terrorism. They have tried to target military action against groups by name, failing to recognize that names change as easily as email addresses. They have tried to "wage a war on terror" using surrogates to carry the fight forward, not realizing that the surrogates do not have the assets or the determination to be successful. They have argued that as long as we keep terrorism out of the US we will be safe, not realizing that such a policy is an open invitation for every terrorist in the world to make an attempt to carry out an attack here. Politicians are looking to the next election while terrorist are looking to the next generation. Unfortunately, the solution to terror is not political (other than political courage to face reality), but is military in nature. No matter how effective a "bombing campaign" might be at denying terrorists freedom of motion or meeting their logistic support requirements, the only way to end a terror threat is to eliminate terrorists. Unfortunately that means one-on-one, face-to-face confrontation between the "good guys" and the "bad guys". In short, "boots on the ground" is the only realistic solution.

Over the recent past (2009-2015), there has been a growing effort to reduce the size and capabilities of the American military presence in a world that has grown progressively more dangerous. The terror threat that was once generally contained in limited portions of the middle-east has grown to now operate freely in much wider regions of the middle-east and Africa. Terror attacks now occur with regularity in all areas of the world and the threats of attack are constant. So while America and its allies have grown less capable, terror has grown stronger and spread. The job of destroying the terror threat grows each day while our capacity and resolve seem to wane. Equally significant is the growing number of nations that openly or covertly support terror activities and the lack of international response.

The answer is simple but executing it is anything but simple. America must take the leadership role in conducting positive military action against terror groups wherever they may be. That action must continue until terror no longer is a threat to the peaceful nations of the world. The action must include effective economic sanctions or direct military actions against any and all nations that support or harbor terror groups or terrorist activities. America cannot carry on this fight alone but America must lead the way and set a positive example for the rest of the world. To do anything else will lead to the eventual failure of the great American experiment and the elimination of America as a power for good on the world scene. There really is no other choice.

K is for K-12 Education

Personal education is a matter of personal responsibility and directly linked to an individual's ability to create self-reliance and self-dependence. Similarly, it is the direct personal responsibility of a parent to provide their children with the education necessary to properly function in our society. For an individual to do any less is to deprive themselves of the opportunities available and to destine their children to a life of poverty and denial.

While citizens may assign to states a responsibility to "provide for the education of all children or citizens" that assignment does not relieve the parent of assuring the actual education of their children. The state cannot and should not ever be allowed to usurp a parent's right and responsibility for providing a proper education for their children.

A parent has a right to choice regarding the manner in which their children will be educated. They may accept the responsibility of education through "home schooling". They may elect to enroll their children in a private educational system and bear the expense associated with that choice. They may elect to rely on the public school system but in doing so they do not surrender their right to demand a quality education for the children. Regardless of the means of education, there must be a universally accepted minimum level of outcome demanded. The advancement and completion of basic education, commonly the K-12 schooling, must produce a graduate that is competent in the basic living skills of reading, writing, math, science, civics, the arts, and the routine demands of being an active participant of society. Each graduate of the basic education system should be prepared for and capable of obtaining and holding a job that will be life sustaining, offer opportunity for advancement, and provide for an appropriate life style in society. Each individual should be fully capable of expressing their thoughts and ideas in clear writing or oral discussion.

For those who desire to gain education beyond the normal K-12 progression, the basic education programs must offer the opportunity to make proper preparation. Individuals should be prepared so that they are able to enter into advanced education without the need for remedial education in basic areas such as reading, writing, math, or basic sciences. Individuals seeking higher education should have the necessary learning and study skills that will allow them to succeed providing they exert the necessary effort and attention to their studies. Similarly, individuals interested in following a more direct technical field should be properly prepared to enter and succeed at the advanced education associated with that field. The quality of education should not be determined by a grade on a "standardized" test but on the demonstrated ability of the students to demonstrate the "real world" application of that education.

Public education is the responsibility of the local users of the system. The policies and operations of each of the various school districts through each state is placed in the hands of an elected School Board. The individuals elected to that responsibility are not provided an opportunity to "rule" over the education system for the district but are charged with the responsibility of making sure that the basic precepts of a sound basic education are achieved. That Board, not the teacher's union, needs to make the decisions regarding educational policy. The local school district is not the place to "experiment" with advanced educational ideas regarding basic education principles. If that experimentation is necessary, let some other school district take the lead. That is not to say that a school district should not be aware of and incorporate technology advances in the classroom. To the contrary, those advances should be incorporated in the classrooms so long as they do not hamper the ability to present essential educational information or become so burdensome on the budget as to impact on actual educational efforts.

Teachers, in overwhelming majority, are indeed wonderful and giving people. Those who do their jobs exceptionally well should be recognized and rewarded accordingly. After all, if we want excellence in educational outcome, we need to provide clear notice for those who provide that service. On the other hand, some individuals, despite their "calling" and their individual desire to be a good teacher, just do not meet the challenge. Those individuals should be offered the opportunity to use their skills in some arena other than public education. The same guidelines should apply to administrators and others involved in the education system. Either produce the required results or find another field in which to work. These are the very rules that the graduates they will produce will be faced with in life so there is no reason educators should not be held to the same standard.

As individuals, we need to be more directly involved in the near constant changes and revisions being made to our education system by the self-proclaimed education experts. It may be a bit time-worn to bring up the "when I was a kid" discussion but there is great wisdom in that position when it comes to education. The importance of mastering the basics of math, reading, writing, logic, speech, elemental science, and the arts has not changed in the past 200 years. Not surprising, the subject matter to be mastered has not changed much in that time period either. Recent "advances" in teaching theory that would do away with comprehension of math basics in favor of a more general comprehensive problem solving theory approach or abandoning the instruction of handwriting and use of cursive writing in favor of keyboarding and texting are not really "advances". Learning about number systems has its place in the study of math but it should not replace the mastery of the basic understanding of addition, subtraction, multiplication and division. While educators may presume that everyone will always be firmly attached to a keyboard at some point in the future, the ability to use handwriting to express thoughts or present ideas will never be replaced. Handwriting is an essential living skill.

The current educational system seems to want to exclude parents from responsibility rather than demand that parents take responsibility. While parents (and especially grandparents, with appropriate background checks) are welcomed as "volunteers" in most schools, the ideas about education that those parents and grandparents offer are not very welcome. Parents who do not monitor the performance of their children on a near continuous basis only find that problems exist when "performance reports" that they probably don't understand come home. By then time and opportunity to take immediate and effective corrective action has been lost. The system has to be more open to individual parents and citizens who are, after all footing the bill, to have a better understanding of how the system is working, what is being taught and why, and how outcomes are being determined. Parents also need to have better avenues of communications with teachers and administrators so that problems can be more properly addressed at an early stage and corrective action implemented. Something as simple as not having homework turned in on time may harbor a deeper problem of lack of understanding or rebellion. The teacher cannot fix that problem but a parent should.

Finally there is need to address the misguided understanding that self- respect and personal pride can be taught just like any other subject.
Self-respect and pride are earned through personal achievement and not because some other person tries to bestow them upon you. Likewise, you will not show respect for or give your respect to a person who has not earned it. While every person is due some level of respect for simply being a person, that does not mean they can either demand personal respect or expect it to be extended. Certain positions or offices in our society expect that respect will be given because of that position or office. For example, elected officials enjoy the respect for the office but that is not necessarily respect for themselves. Persons older than ourselves are nominally paid respect because of their additional experience in life. Our parents are shown respect for being our parents. A nominal degree of respect for others is extended as a courtesy but that respect can be lost by the individual to whom it has been extended. You, through your actions and accomplishments, earn the respect that you receive from others.

L is for Legislated Rights

Chapter 5 of this book contains a detailed discussion of the "Rights" of man and the manner in which they were given to us and the role of government as a protector of those rights. While the Constitution does not specify every right given to us by our Creator it is very clear that the role of government does not include granting "rights' of any kind to anybody.

In the modern society we continually hear about the "rights" of this group or that or of some individual being violated or infringed upon by some person or society in general. In fact, almost all of our time and effort today is spent addressing the "rights" of others (and perhaps even ourselves). Unfortunately, what we are really doing is attempting to define the actions by government (or demands to government) to legislate special privileges for a group or individual.

The nature of our governmental system and society is that we shall protect the right of all to be treated equally under the law. To that end, governments may legislate privileges to facilitate that protection. Government may legislate that discrimination in the public place is not allowed. Government cannot legislate that no person will discriminate against another, after all the right to form opinion and act on those opinions is an individual right. Government may legislate that education for children shall be provided on an equal basis. Government cannot legislat that the outcome of the education provided will be the same for all children.

Government can legislate the manner in which people may register to vote. Government cannot, through legislation, eliminate or modify the requirement for US Citizenship to vote.

Civil Rights are directly related to equal protection under the law.

There are no "rights" associated with selected sexual preference other than the right to make the choice.

There are no "rights" associated with the termination of pregnancy.

There are no "rights" that guarantee home ownership or ownership of any other private property item

Animals have no "rights" under our system of government.

There is no "right" that assures that a person speaking must be listened to.

There is no "right" to destroy the property of others or public property while exercising the right to assemble peacefully or request redress of grievances.

There is no "right" to refuse to accept the moral and religious beliefs of others simply because they do not match yours or would allow that individual to not embrace your behavior.

There is no "right" to any service or material item provided by another of their own free will nor is there any authority for government to mandate that any or all citizens must purchase that service or material item.

You have the "right" to add to this list of "non-rights" as you see fit.

M is for Medical Care

There was a time in America when "medical" attention was provided by whoever happened to be available and had some basic knowledge or experience in addressing a specific physical malady. Medical doctors, especially the various varieties of "specialists" we have today, were not readily available in most communities or settings. People simply got by as best they could with what they had. The results were frequently a bit less than desired. There was no preconceived notion of a successful outcome for all medical problems and those who made an honest attempt to aid were not held in public contempt or legally responsible when success was not achieved. People actually accepted that not all outcomes would be favorable and that some patients might even die. When doctors were available the patient paid directly for the service provided and barter was a common practice. Not everyone received care from a doctor and not everyone received the same level of care.

In today's world of medical care, expectations are somewhat different. Things have changed significantly both in the availability of high quality medical care and the perception of how that care is to be provided. For some reason, not supported by either logic or fact, there is a growing impression that everyone has a "right" to medical care, that all individuals have a "right" to the same level of care, and that outcomes must be positive. In some instances, the medical profession and its moral code of service have become as big a part of the problem as it has the solution. In addition, government action at various levels has also muddied the waters with respect to health care.

To establish a firm basis, we must be absolutely clear that there is no unalienable right to health care. Health care is provided by an individual who has given of his (or her) time, money, and effort to develop a skill set that is marketable and desired in the community. They have invested in themselves in expectation to earn a reasonable return on that investment. They offer a service, based on their education and experience, to the public and expect a

161

payment from the public in return for that service. Because the service they offer is, in fact, private property (intellectual property which they own) they have every right to set the price for their services. The doctor also has a right to determine who gets treated and under what circumstances. Of course, because the medical profession, as a whole, recognizes a moral obligation to serve all and to not ignore those in immediate need of attention, a problem in the delivery model has been created.

In general, no doctor would refuse their service or ability to aid a person in an immediate life threatening situation. Doctors have answered the call for need first and worried about payment later. Those who required the immediate assistance of a doctor, received that aid even if they were unable to pay. It was what being a doctor was all about. Doctors were also more generally tied to the families that they served and the title or term "family doctor" long preceded the current term of "primary care provider". The family doctor attended to the general health of the members of the family from birth until death.

With the advent of larger communities and a growing health care system, coupled with the recognition of the value of a skilled medical approach to trauma and an effective means of transporting victims from the scene of an accident to a care facility, hospital emergency rooms came into existence and became very efficient. For people suffering major trauma or medical incidents, the care at an "emergency room" often resulted in life over death. The emergency room did not turn patients away and the manner in which payment would be made was determined after treatment was completed. The very fact that "emergency room" meant immediate (or guaranteed) medical assistance eventually resulted in those with no family doctor or those who knew they were unable to pay for medical service to turn to the emergency room as their primary medical service provider. Concurrently, government using the police power of licensing, began to regulate the actions of medical service providers and soon legislated that Emergency Rooms could not turn away potential patients even if they had no means of payment. That governmental position soon found its way into the court system when individuals who did not receive the treatment they thought they deserved or for whom the emergency room outcome was not as they desired, filed suit against doctors and hospitals for various failures and misconducts.

Compounding the growth of legislation and legal recourse, was the significant increase in the demand for medical assistance. There was a time in the not too distant past when "take two aspirin and call me in the morning" was the appropriate answer to a small medical problem. Not every illness (real or perceived) warranted a visit to the doctor and certainly not the emergency room. Individuals were not constantly bombarded with information about new "wonder" drugs that could cure all aliments and recommendations to "ask your doctor about.....". We did not have an internet to allow the growth of self-diagnosis, which is interesting because we want the person with years of education and experience to be infallible but place great faith in something we found on the internet.
Most recently, in an effort to make sure that all Americans had access to health care, the federal government adopted the "Affordable Care Act....(ACA)" also known as Obama Care. Under the provisions of this federal mandate, all persons are required to be covered by some form of health insurance and failure to have coverage makes the individual subject to a fine disguised as a tax. By its very nature ACA makes it clear that medical care is not an unalienable right but is a requirement mandated by government. The primary questions of "where in the Constitution is government delegated the authority to mandate for individuals to purchase anything, much less medical care?", and "where in the Constitution is government delegated the authority to direct and regulate the use of the intellectual property of medical care providers?", seem to be lost or ignored in the continuing discussion. The most significant detriment to the government action in the case of the ACA is not the unwarranted takeover of our medical care system but, rather, the foundation that has been laid for government to impose its will on any segment of our lives it may so desire. Did we not have a small dust up in 1776 over the same concerns about government excess?

163

One of the most common arguments supporting government takeover is the need to provide medical care to all and that there is no other way to make it happen. Absolutely false. The assumptions that everyone has the right to equal care, every outcome will be favorable to the patient, and that cost will never be a consideration in providing care make no sense and are contrary to sound logic. It is true that all people should have access to medical care. It is not true that equal medical care can or should be provided to all. There is no way to make that happen. It is true that medical personnel should use sound judgement and the highest level of skill (commensurate with their training) to provide care and treatment to patients. It is not true that all medical treatment will or should have a successful outcome as determined by the patient or their relatives. Medicine is as much an art as a science and the human body is not some mechanical device that responds favorable to part replacement or simple ministrations. Medical "miracles" may occur but they are not the basis for determining "proper medical care". It is not true that cost cannot and should not be a factor in providing medical care. This has nothing to do with the "value" of a human life but it does have everything to do with the allocation of resources. A basic understanding of human life is that it ends, most frequently without our ability to influence that reality. While medical professionals have a moral obligation (self-imposed) to "first, do no harm", they do not have an obligation to take all steps possible to sustain the life of an individual. While it may not seem "fair" (news flash – life is not fair) that some can afford better care than others, that is a fact of life. If it were not we would all be living in mansions and driving a Maserati.

The reality is that we each will get the medical care we can afford (and normally a lot more) but there is a limit and we do not have a right to demand beyond our means. In the end, pay-as-you-go or health insurance that reflects both the needs and ability to pay, are the correct answer to the health care problem. Most certainly, government intervention and mandate are not the correct answer.

N is for Nanny State

It was never the intent of the founding fathers that individuals should be dependent on the state for any reason. The entire concept of our national being is that we would individually act to provide for our individual needs and would act in concert with others for the provision of limited common ends. The very basic premise of the American way of life is that people shall always be free of the controlling mantle of any government and shall exercise and enjoy the maximum extent of liberty possible to any people.

Another guiding principle of the American way of life is that we will, to the extent possible and appropriate, see to our own needs and to provide for those less fortunate in life. The achievement of the "American Dream" may not be possible for all but those who do achieve that level generally understand that they had help along the way and return the favor in kind. The support of those still struggling and striving for full self-dependence through direct assistance and community service organizations is a part of the American way. Conservatives are well known for their generous outreach to offer the helping hand. Those personal efforts, made as a matter of choice and executed through non-governmental avenues, are the conservative way.

In today's America, we find government, at all levels, functioning to "provide" for the needs of those defined as "in poverty" or "needy". In reality, what government is actually doing is providing a minimum level of support for classes and groups of people created by that same government. Before the advent of the various welfare and social provider programs, individuals worked hard and did whatever it took to provide for themselves and their families. The family functioned as a unit for self-dependence and that cohesive effort endured across generations. There was no thought of expecting government to "pay the bills". Once progressive government decided that bringing all people out of poverty and that leveling the economic status of all individuals was not only within their power but a primary duty of government, the massive downhill slide began.

Individuals understand the value of individual effort and the need to make their own way in the world. If they want to eat they need to earn the food. If they want shelter from the cold or the storm they need to earn that shelter. Except for a limited few who selected a lifestyle that was well outside the social norm, most individuals had the basic desire to be a functioning part of society. Individuals had a level of self-respect that would not allow them to become wards of the community. They found a way to contribute to the community. If they needed a place to sleep, they traded hard work for a night in the barn. If they were hungry, they traded hard work for a meal. Seldom was begging for anything acceptable to either the beggar or society. Sleeping on sidewalks, panhandling on street corners, or stealing food or other private property were simply not acceptable to society and not resorted to by the majority of those in need. The most in need found a way to contribute and, in return, the community found a way to assist them in achieving their life goals. The community provided the hand up rather than the hand out.

A lesson learned in life is that a dependency once established is very hard to break. When government began to provide direct support to those in the lower economic strata of society there is no doubt it was conceived as a good idea with honorable intent. What was missed was that if you start to feed people they soon lose the ability and incentive to feed themselves. When housing is provided, even if it is not the very best, it is better than what they were able to afford and the cost was now zero. Who would not want to take advantage of the offer? Unfortunately, along with lost incentive there was also a loss of self-respect and a loss of respect for the "free" home. It did not take long for the individual, now on direct support from the government, to accept that support as a "right" and begin to demand more to improve their social well-being. The power of the welfare class became evident in the ballot box and soon those living on the hard labor of others were beginning to dictate, through their elected representatives, both the nature and extent of the support they were due. They became the ultimate takers in a society that set the stage for their failure. Families fractured, out of wedlock birth and single parent families became widely accepted, education faltered because it was no longer necessary for economic wellbeing, and children with no viable role models simply slipped into second and third generation welfare recipient families. What was started with perhaps very good intent actually produced a social disaster. And today, the progressive intent is to continue to grow the number of individuals living in a government dependent world.

The conservative response to the situation is straight-forward and simple. Stop making individuals dependent on government. First and foremost, establish and maintain a basic education system that provides each and every citizen with the knowledge necessary to survive and, if they desire, prosper in our America. Second, no person able to work and provide a useful product for the community will be eligible to receive any kind of government subsistence support without first engaging in that work. The level of subsistence will be comparable to the work output. The period of subsistence will be limited and closely associated with a period for education and training to make the individual self-sufficient. Third, stop rewarding procreation by making payments for additional babies born out of wedlock or without visible means of support from a father. Under current law, a woman cannot be denied the ability to exercise her "right" to obtain appropriate means of controlling unwanted pregnancy. It would seem appropriate that, as a term of receiving any government largess, the woman would agree to prevent pregnancy. Further, should a pregnancy occur, the mother would have to identify the father in order to continue to receive government support. Finally, because there is a direct correlation between poverty and poor education and between both of those essentials and imprisonment as the result of criminal activity, the approach to prison service must change. A person serving a sentence in prison is doing so at the will and direction of the state. Prison time will be used to gain an education and learn a viable trade. Society (and not the prisoners) will operate the prisons.

167

Gangs will not be allowed to thrive and prisons will no longer serve as recruiting centers for future criminal or terrorist activity. For those individuals confined to prison who are deemed incorrigible, they shall be isolated in separate institutions that, while preserving all of their basic rights, eliminate all of the privileges associated with a free and open society. The monetary cost to society might be high in the initial years but the end result will be a significant savings in both money and reclaimed people. The outcome of a stay in a prison must be a firm sense of personal responsibility, self-discipline, and self-respect. If those are not gained the time in prison has been wasted.

O is for Ownership of Private Property and Property Rights

To achieve an understanding of the significance of property rights in the United States and the importance of those rights to a free economy, a short review of our national beginnings is necessary.

The United States, derived initially from the peaceful association of thirteen prior colonies of the British Empire, and added to since inception, is unique in both its origin and its governing precepts. The British Empire, from which the colonies gained their freedom by force of arms, was a democratic monarchy with major power vested in the monarch under the concept of the divine rights of kings. That form of government proclaimed that all power flowed from God to kings on earth and that kings then relegated power to their people only as they so desired. The link to the British Empire as a predecessor for the United States is important.

The government of the British Empire, and specifically England, was itself the product of a revolution of the people against the monarchy. In 1215, the Barons, merchants, and clergy, along with other elements of English population, objecting to ever increasing taxation levied by the Monarchy, rose up against King John and forced a major revision in the power of the Monarch and the rights of the people. The Magna Carta (Great Charter) signed by King John, for the first time formally overcame the concept of the divine rights of Kings and guaranteed rights to Englishmen that could not be rescinded or overridden by the throne. Among the rights established was that of private citizens to own and control the use of real property. Significant in the extension of property rights under Magna Carta was the absence of any ability by the owners to control taxation of the property by the throne or any real limitation on the right of the throne to "temporarily" make use of the property in the best interest of the Empire. Regardless, the right of private property ownership was established as a continuing part of English law. Important to that relationship was that all property not in specific private ownership was the property of the crown and could

169

be obtained only through the willingness of the crown. Such was the case when the colonies were founded on the American continent.

Although North America was colonized by several European states and many states laid claim to various parts of the continent over time, the thirteen colonies that were to become the United States all fell under the rule of the English King. English law became the law of the colonies and, although some local government control was authorized by the crown, all significant decisions impacting the colonies remained with Parliament and the crown. Through a series of actual and contrived miscues by the crown, aided by the actions of a number of colonial activists seeking local rule, relationships with England deteriorated to the point that secession from the Empire and armed revolt became inevitable. Following commencement of armed hostilities, in order to establish independence as the ultimate goal of the colonies, our Declaration of Independence was penned. That document established why we exist as a separate nation and documented the basis of who we are and what we stand for. The Declaration of Independence took Americans one major step further down the path of defining the origin of the rights of citizens.

Our Declaration of Independence, the most unique document of its type in the history of the world, boldly established that the rights of the people flowed from the creator and not the King. This massive departure from historical precedence, common law, and the theory of the divine rights of Kings, resulted in a completely new association of the people and their government. Before the Declaration of Independence, all power was vested in the Monarch who relegated and extended certain rights to the people. Under that form of people/government relationship, all rights not specifically granted to the people by the crown were, without reservation or limit, strictly reserved to the crown. With the Declaration of Independence, the role was reversed and, from that point forward, government would have only the power and authority granted to it by the people. The codification of that principle is found in the Constitution of the United States.

The principle of private ownership of property was so important to the founding fathers that The Paris Peace Treaty of 1783, which ended the American Revolution, went to great lengths to restore the private property of those who remained loyal to the King during the conflict. The process included the states repaying those who purchased confiscated property to ensure that it was fully restored without loss to either party. That action provides a clear indication of the understanding of the importance of private ownership and the responsibility of government to protect the rights of ownership.

The preamble of the US Constitution clearly identifies that the government is the creation of the people. Within the Constitution, the specific powers and authorities extended to government by the people, are enumerated and limited. Further, the Constitution is complete and firm in the role of government in preserving the rights of the people and the reservation to the people all rights not specifically granted to government. Further strengthening the impact of the Constitution is the care and effort extended by the framers to make it a clearly readable simple document not subject to misunderstanding as to its intent and meaning. The Constitution of the United States reserves the right of property ownership to the people and charges government to protect that right. The wording of the Fifth Amendment that "No person …. Shall be deprived of life, liberty, or property without due process of law; nor shall private property be taken for public use without just compensation" clearly establishes the protected right of property ownership. It follows that, under the American system of government, since all power flows from the creator to the people and since the people have not assigned the right or authority of ownership of all property to government, the right of ownership of private property, endowed on the people by the creator, is fully retained by the people.

Real estate or land is a special case of private property because it is immobile, indestructible, and fully unique. That very uniqueness provides for the specific interest in property ownership to be defined in a "Bundle of Rights" including;

171

1. The right to control the property (within the law)

2. The right to enjoy the property (in any legal manner)

3. The right to control access to the property (as defined by the legal rights of a property owner)

4. The right to legally dispose of the property in part or in whole.

Of particular note, these basic rights were clearly understood and correctly considered by the framers of our Constitution. The Constitution specifically protects against improper search and seizure (right to control access protected), deprivation of property without due process (right to control, enjoy and dispose), forced housing of soldiers (right to access). Further, the Constitution does not grant to government the power to ignore or legislate contrary to property rights because "The enumeration in the Constitution, of certain rights, shall not be construed to deny or disparage others retained by the people".

Having firmly established that property ownership is a right of the people and not a privilege extended by government or a right controlled by government, it is worthwhile to understand the real underlying importance of the issue. Real property is the source of all economic wealth.

Wealth, in an economic sense, is created when a product or service is produced that is desired by others and thus subject to trade. The value placed on the trade item is generally consistent with the desire or need for the trade item. Products are the direct result of extraction of a natural resource from property, with value added by labor and/or process. Without the available natural resources of property, creation of wealth is not possible. The natural resources of property include every possible use and are inherent in the rights of property ownership. Thus the value of property is based on the natural resources that it contains and the ability to use those resources. In considering the common economic wealth of any individual or nation, it is not possible to define that wealth except in terms of basic natural resources of property. An argument that "intellectual" property creates wealth without impact on natural resources is not correct. Try as we might, it would be nearly impossible to identify an intellectual property that is offered to the world that is not dependent , in some way, on another product that is the product of property natural resources. Books need to be printed to realize value. Software requires a computer for operation. A play needs a stage and actors to be presented. Individual thoughts need some media to be presented and preserved.

Because property is the central element in economic wealth, it follows that any restriction on the exercise of the "bundle of rights" of property ownership, and most specifically, any restriction on the enjoyment of use of the property, will result in a decrease in the value of the property. Under the United States Constitution, when such devaluation is the result of government action, a "take" has occurred and compensation may be in order. It is also of specific interest to understand that government is limited to "taking" private property for public use and that the term "public good" is not contained within the Constitution. Thus, by definition, government may not exercise power of eminent domain to obtain private property it then passes to another private owner. Similarly, adopting land use regulations for "common good" or "public good" have no basis in the Constitution. If enacted, those regulations must be subject to the same parameters as a "taking" for public use, subject to the same lawful process and subject to the same compensation requirements.

P is for Prejudice (in General)

There can be no doubt that America as a nation and as a society has and still does, to a very small degree, exercise prejudice with respect to race, creed, and ethnic origin. In America, the exercise of bigotry is very limited and finds itself in a very small part of the populace that relies on its bigoted philosophy as the basis for their continued existence. The existence of prejudice is not unique to America. It is prevalent around the world. The global condition does not excuse or explain the existence of prejudice in America but it does lend some understanding to the continuation of its existence. Prejudice is not limited to a single race or creed but exists in all units of society.

That said, it is just as significant to note that America is not a nation of prejudice or bigotry. There is no documented proof for any such claim and using historical reference that was cleared over 100 years ago is a false argument. Those who continue to make the argument that decedents of people who were enslaved have a right to more opportunity or that they continue to be limited in opportunity today makes no sense. Those who would attempt to use any event that crosses racial lines to further the hatred of bigotry should be soundly condemned in the public square by all. "Race baiters," and those who attempt to foster unrest, are friends to none.

America is a nation of immigrants. Our shores have been crossed by peoples fleeing oppression, hunger, or tyranny across the globe. Many have arrived with little more than the clothes on their backs. Some have arrived against their will and been held in bondage. Over time, as a people we have worked hard to rectify the ills that existed in society. America was one of the first countries to outlaw slavery of humans and extend our protection to peoples around the world. American has led the way in the elimination of institutional prejudice through law and direct legal action. In general, the people of America have opened their doors and their hearts to people in need regardless of race, creed or ethnic origin. All that said, prejudice still exists and more work must be done.

Those who espouse "political correctness" do great harm to the ability of the nation to address and resolve any divides that exist. America, as a nation, is one of assimilation rather than division. While early settlers and inhabitants had their differences, they came to appreciate that mutual cooperation and respect resulted in reaching a common good. Our forefathers and the individuals who gave of their fortunes, honor, and lives to create this nation fully understood that those who lived in this nation were Americans. While some of the customs and memories of the past and of the countries they came from were retained by Americans, their first allegiance was to America. Becoming an American and improving their way of life was the most important consideration for people coming to this country. There were no hyphenated anything's; there were only Americans.

The effort today, led by progressives, to separate and divide people into small sub groups that affiliate based on ethnic origin, creed, race, or gender is absolutely contrary to the principle upon which America was founded and contrary to the best interest of every individual so influenced. We have divided the country into so many different interest groups and made virtually everyone a "victim" of the actions or ideas of someone else that it is hard to find a single "American" in our midst. No person is safe from being charged a bigot, homophobe, misogynist, racist, or anti-something as the result of a simple statement of opinion. We have taken to personal and character assassination as a way of debate and forgotten the ability to communicate ideas openly and freely. It has become more important to be a hyphenated something than to be an American. "What's in it for me?" has been the response to every proposal made by any level of government or any program under discussion. "I have a right to---" has replaced the principle of "I have a personal responsibility to---". Long gone is the idea John Kennedy espoused when he advised us to "Ask not what your country can do for you, ask what you can do for your country". When did rioting in the streets and destruction of private and public property become the common response to a disagreement with a police action or the success or failure of a sports team? When did America become a nation of minorities rather than a nation of individuals striving for a common purpose? When did the principles put forth by Adams, Jefferson, Henry, Hamilton, and Madison become corrupted by the dissention offered today by the likes of Jackson, Sharpton, Schumer, and Olinsky? How can we ever hope to find common ground for discussion and resolution of differences if we refuse to even respect the positions of each other?

R is for Resistance and Assembly (Civil Disobedience)

Civil Disobedience and civil protest are elemental to America as a nation. It was through various acts of civil disobedience that the colonists expressed their displeasure with the acts of the British crown with respect to the rule of the colonies. The initial civil disobedience grew to a war of revolution and armed conflict that earned the freedom of the colonies to exercise self-government. Throughout the history of the nation, civil disobedience from the "Whiskey Rebellion" in 1791, through the civil rights marches of the 1960's and beyond, has been a part of the force that has changed the nation. The significance of civil discord was so significant that the founding fathers gave it specific protection in **"Congress shall make no law…abridging the freedom of speech,,…., or the right of the people to peaceably assemble and petition the Government for the redress of grievances"** (Amendment 1). It is clear that the right to speak and assemble (the primary elements of civil discord) are among the unalienable rights granted by our Creator.

Civil discord, by its very nature, will be a condition of disagreement among peoples. There will be at least two sides to the debate that is the subject of the discord. Without those differences, the need for debate and the resultant discord would not be present. Principle to the understanding of discord is that it will be peaceful in its inception and conduct and will always respect the unalienable rights of others. The clear line between civil discord and riot is the impact of the assembly on the rights of other.

Over time, the limitations on the ability of the people to assemble peacefully have been subject to limits imposed, before the fact, by society as a whole. Unrestricted parades in the streets in the 1800's that had little or no real impact on the economic viability of the community went generally unchecked. Carry your sign, chant your slogan, and parade through the streets to try to convince others of the correctness of your point of view. However, when the gatherings and parades began to have direct impact on other persons or the general activities of the community, such as business or general transportation, society decided to impose a few rules or regulations. These were not about the ability to commit civil discord but about the time and places where such discord was not appropriate. In general, the system has worked with some reasonable degree of success. Small gatherings and demonstrations are precluded from having major impact on the routine life of the community. Major assemblies and demonstrations, however, still are able to fill the streets with the concerned to make their position known.

Not all civil disobedience is appropriate or consistent with the concepts of self-discipline, integrity and the requirement inherent in the protection of rights for all. The right to assemble and protest does not include the refusal to honor and respect the rights of all others. Civil disobedience does not include open violent actions toward those assigned the responsibility to protect the members of society and to assure the peace of the community. Open violent action against lawfully appointed officers of the law is not civil disobedience but is criminal activity. Failure to follow the instructions of police officers who are acting within the capacity of their office and executing the duties of that office is also criminal activity on the part of the protestors. Doing damage to private property, including local businesses, looting, setting fires, overturning cars, tearing down street lamps, and all those other activities that have become more common with recent "civil protest" are all illegal and directly violate the rights of others. More significant is that the number of injuries and even deaths that have occurred during modern day "protests" are reprehensible and have no protections under the Constitution or the law. The person or persons responsible for any injury or death not directly related to enforcement of the law, are violators of the law and should be punished. Those individuals who would use the pretext and cover of honest acts of mass civil disobedience to serve as a cover for their illegal activities should be exposed by the community and brought to justice.

If the purpose of civil disobedience is to make others and the government aware of perceived or actual wrongs being committed to individuals, the objective of that disobedience should be to change minds and achieve redress of the wrongs. That end result will seldom, if ever, be achieved through open aggressive violent action. When all else fails, the acts of civil disobedience should result in significant issues that are resolved through the ballot box.

S is for Social Security

In the interest of clarity and being straight on this issue, I must declare that I am a Social Security recipient. I came under the Social Security program early in my service in the military when the government decided to offset some of the cost of military retirement by enrolling all military members in the program. I paid my payroll taxes just like every other American worker. Perhaps one difference is that my eventual military retirement pay was reduced by an amount equal to or approximating the Social Security payments. It could be argued that although I receive a Social Security check it is really nothing more than an earned military retirement supplement.

In the wake of the economic disaster experienced by many American workers and their families in the stock market crash of 1929 and the associated bank failures, the federal government enacted the social security legislation. The purpose of the social security program was to provide for persons in retirement or disabled and unable to work as well as the mothers and children in the event of the death of the family bread winner. The program, as designed, was to be funded by dedicated taxes paid by the individuals and their employers. The taxes collected were to be placed in a "trust" fund that could only be used to make payments to those authorized to receive benefits under the social security program. Social security was the first nation-wide social welfare program implemented by the federal government and at the time was intended to be a strictly limited program. Like so many good intentioned efforts by a federal government that over reaches its authority, Social Security became the cornerstone for the federal social welfare system that we know today. What was a relatively simple and well-intended program has grown to be the single greatest draw on the federal treasury.

It is interesting to note that Medicare, the plan to support basic health services for the elderly, was in fact considered an insurance program. Workers paid into the system through payroll tax deductions across the entire period of their employment. Upon retirement (reaching the specified retirement age) limited basic health benefits were available to the individual. The individual visited their doctor and the federal government paid some part of or all of the medical bill. The program was limited but did provide basic health coverage. The Medicare program has all of the markings of the Healthcare savings account proposals that have been offered in recent years and so thoroughly discredited by progressives. It is a bit hard to reconcile how a federal program that requires set tax payments for limited future services is any different, let alone superior, to a program that allows the individual to select the level of payment and the level of service desired and to do so in a savings account.

The Social Security Trust Fund, into which all Social Security and Medicare tax payments were to be placed, was formed on paper and continues to exist today. Congress and the President found that the Trust fund was a reasonable source of funds for normal operation of the federal government and, consequentially, social security tax dollars were "borrowed" and replaced with paper debit vouchers. The very funds that were to be invested to help provide for the future of the fund were instead diverted to cover other government "expenses". The trust was a simple place to "borrow" from because there was no outside investor and no bonds or notes that came due on a date certain or subject to call from the investor. It was a short time before the funds available in the trust were insufficient to cover the current liabilities (payments to those currently retired or eligible for payments) and to establish the investment account necessary to provide for future beneficiaries. In short, instead of being paid from invested funds they had paid into the trust, beneficiaries were being paid from taxes being paid by current workers. Thus the death spiral began. While it might appear that a simple solution of having the government simply repay the loans to the social security trust would solve the problem, there was no practical way to make that work. Federal spending had grown beyond the actual means of the taxes collected annually and the government began a process of continuous borrowing to pay the bills. That annual borrowing included using the funds from Social

Security trust in excess of the annual benefit payments. To reverse the spending and borrowing habits, congress and the President would have had to stop taking funds from the Trust (requiring a significant general spending reduction), and then either curtail spending further or borrow from another source to acquire the dollars necessary to replenish the Trust. That has not happened.

To make the process and what went wrong a bit more clear, let's take the family savings example. Mom and Dad along with each of the kids, agree to place a certain amount of their monthly wages in a family savings account. The money is there to earn interest and will not be used except to pay a monthly stipend to each contributing member when they retire. The stipend amount will be based on the amount paid in over the period of time. This is a reasonably simple system. The number of contributors grows as additional children and grandchildren enter the work force and the interest earned grows as the account gets bigger. The basic system has every potential to work for as long as the family may desire. Then comes the deal breaker. Dad (he is always our bad guy,) or someone else paying into the fund, decides they need some immediate cash to buy something they want right now. They may either "borrow" some funds from the account (without the knowledge of others – this is after all a TRUST account) or may just "defer" payment for a bit. The value of the account declines and does not grow as programmed and the interest earned is reduced. If the "loan" or short payments are not repaid quickly (worse yet, never repaid) the account begins to operate in a deficit (compared to expected) position. If the borrowed and delayed payment option is exercised to any major extent, the fund will fail and the end users will be left with no return on their investment and no stipend in retirement. That is the condition of the Social Security Trust.

With the tax revenues no longer able to fund the current and future obligations of the system, a significant effort was made to reform the entire Social Security system. That effort entailed expanding the number and classes of beneficiaries of payments for the social security trust without significant increase in the tax base for the trust. Disability programs were added to the program and continuously expanded. Payments were increased to account for inflation and then sustained by annual "cost of living increases". The categories of people eligible to receive benefits under both Social Security payments and Medicare continued to increase and the health coverage under Medicare broadened. The individual taxes increased but still were unable to cope with the current and future costs of the system. The Social Security obligation, represented by a debt for government, continued to grow.

In 2008 approximately 51 million Americans (or persons residing in the US) received about 615 Billion dollars in social security payouts. That averages approximately 1000 dollars a month for each recipient. Perhaps more telling is that the entire work force supporting that Social Security tax system was something less than 154 million workers. It becomes readily apparent that the system is not sustainable and will crash financially in the foreseeable future. Common sense and basic math make the end result clear.

The Social Security system, as originally designed, would meet with conservative approval and support. Individual persons were investing their personal funds (even if collected as a tax) into a security account that they could draw on in their retirement years. Ignoring the fact that there was no "means testing" of the program (who would actually need the support) at the front end or at the delivery end, the program was generally an acceptable idea. This was a program that had individuals exercising personal responsibility for their future well-being (even if the government was the executing agent). The Social Security system has strayed far from that conservative approach. The system has been expanded without commensurate and appropriate contribution (taxes) by future beneficiaries. The system was doomed to fiscal failure when the trust fund became a limitless slush fund for Congress and the President with no reasonable way for repayment or restoration of the funds collected.

As we stand today, the Social Security system represents a major financial debt for America and a social dilemma. The system is not sustainable. The system has degraded from using previously paid funds to a pay-as-you-go system relying on current collected tax dollars. Today it takes the payroll (Social Security) taxes of between 3 to 5 workers to support the payments made to one beneficiary. As the beneficiary pool grows and the labor force shrinks, the ratio of workers to beneficiaries will only get worse. There comes a time when the individuals drawing on the fund and the payments required exceed the payments made by the few who are paying into the fund. At that point the system crashes. Government will be forced to reduce benefits to some or all, borrow money from another source to pay benefits, divert money from other federal programs to support Social Security payments, or, as is most likely for a federal program, levy a huge tax increase somewhere to cover the deficit. In any case, by not addressing the problem yesterday, we have a problem we will not address today and a problem that will ruin us financially tomorrow.

One of the most logical solutions for the social security problem is to offer an alternative to the existing tax contributions to the trust in return for some level of return in the future. Allowing individuals to invest some part or all of their normal social security tax dollars in a personal retirement fund has many advantages and only one major drawback. As with any investment there is a level of risk involved. However the performance history of the stock, bond, and real estate markets has been one of relative stability and growth. There must be some reasonable level of security in the Personal investment idea considering the government is a major supporter of the IRA and 401K retirement plan systems which are essentially personal investment accounts. The federal government sees, in that option, a major problem because the tax dollars would not be collected and held by the US Treasury and would therefore not be readily available for loan and diversion to other government spending. No matter the common sense attached to the more conservative individual retirement account idea, the overwhelming need of government to fund its pet programs will never allow the concept to be put into action. Government, through its shortsighted greed, will deny the American people the right to be self–sufficient and to exercise personal responsibility. The American people, because of their apparent desire to let government be responsible for the major decisions in their lives, appear unwilling to demand positive corrective action or to elect representatives who will champion and bring forth that corrective action.

T is for Taxation

As conservatives we understand the relationship between fair and proper taxation and sound government. We will always endeavor to champion and support proper and appropriate taxation for the government we created. To that end we will always recognize that government cannot and will not grow beyond the limits established by the people unless taxes are collected in excess of actual requirements and then improperly applied to growth of government. We will challenge abuse of taxation authority at every turn.

Taxation is surrounded by a never ending discussion that more frequently is based on perception and emotion than on fact. In the United States, taxes are established by the people to pay for the specific government services that they have authorized through the very same documents that created their governments. The US Constitution specifically authorizes (and limits) Congress "to lay and collect Taxes, Duties, Imposts, and Excises to pay the debts and provide for the common Defense and general Welfare of the United States the collection of taxes….". It follows that the collection of taxes and other fees are to be used to execute the powers delegated to Congress and the Federal government and no other purpose. State Constitutions have similar provisions that authorize the collection of taxes to carry out delegated responsibilities. In addition, citizens in local jurisdictions may create special taxing districts (school districts, fire districts, and park districts are some examples) to provide for services not delegated to the state or local jurisdiction governments. In the case of multiple separate local taxing districts, it is appropriate to understand that no more than one local district may impose tax for a specific end purpose.

With an understanding of the authority delegated to government to collect and use tax and fee funds, it is easier to understand the underlying facts in the ongoing debate. Conservatives support the collection of taxes in a manner and amount that is necessary for government to complete its assigned responsibilities in an effective and efficient manner. Conservatives do not support collection or use of taxes and fees that are used by government to carry out responsibilities or duties that have not been specifically delegated to that government. This then involves an understanding of the limits of delegated responsibility and the never ending efforts by elected representatives and the appointed bureaucracies they have created to seek every expanding power and control. Conservatives find that by limiting the taxing power of government, government will also be limited.

To better understand the frustration of conservatives in regard to inappropriate taxation, let us consider some primary examples.

There has been a long standing debate about the appropriateness of "earmarked" funds by Congress to dedicate funds to a specific project or use in a particular congressional district or state. The Progressives argue that this is a way to make sure that each district or state "gets its fair share" of the federal tax dollars collected and that critical projects in those respective areas are funded. Conservatives argue that there is no provision in the Constitution for "earmarks", that the funds being "earmarked" do not meet the criteria for general budget consideration, that the projects or uses being funded may or may not be within the authority delegated to the federal government, and that the "earmarked" funds represent taxes collected in excess of actual need. So long as the "earmark" system continues it serves little purpose other than for incumbents to "buy votes" by "bringing the bacon home" and imposing an excess tax burden on the people. If the projects or uses of the funds set aside in "earmarks" were actually required in the district or state, why would not the state or district already be funding that project or use?

The Federal Department of Education is allocated tax dollars to support education programs across the nation. Because of the nature of the bureaucratic beast, a significant portion of the "education" dollars are consumed at the federal level to support the Department and the various offices that deal with the identification and design of programs to be supported, the distribution of education funds to states and districts, and the monitoring and oversight of the uses and programs for which the funds were allocated. There is no provision in the Constitution for Congressional responsibility for education. In fact, it has been a long-standing approach to education that basic education shall be provided and controlled at the local level. That approach recognizes the specific importance of the parents in providing for the education of their children and serves as a continuing measure to prevent the takeover of the education system by a central power. The reality of the current federal education support system is that a portion of taxes collected from local districts may be returned to those districts with the provisions that certain federal programs or guidelines be followed or that certain "standards" be met by the local district. The federal government is using the allocation of taxes to coerce local jurisdictions into following federal direction. Failure to comply with the federal program specifications by the local district or state can result the allocated federal dollars being withheld. Such a system is doubly outside the spirit and intent of the Constitution.

Federal tax dollars collected for the supposed purpose of "Transportation" are most frequently used to "assist" local and state governments in adopting central planning programs that have little or nothing to do with actual transportation. One major example is the central planning goal of creating "urban areas" that provide essentially all services to the residents, include the proper mix of lodging and work places, and significantly reduce or eliminate the need for private automobiles. If the local jurisdictions are in compliance with the federal "thoughts" about urban development, they are rewarded by federal dollars for "transportation" projects. Far too often the approved projects have more to do with mass transit, light and heavy rail systems, walking paths, and bike lanes and trails. The use of federal dollars to support construction and maintenance of roads and bridges, a delegated local government responsibility, is very limited. As with other federal funding programs, the "slice of the pie" that is retained by the controlling bureaucracies is considerable and is lost to the original purpose of the tax.

The common denominator in each of these examples is a combined overreach by the federal government and a loss of effective use of funds. If the federal government did not collect the taxes for purposes outside their authority and allowed those funds to be collected and used locally, the effective use would be much higher and more consistent with local desires and needs. In addition, if the federal government did not collect the funds there would no need for "departments" and "administrations" exercising extra constitutional authority. Budgeting would be more simple, Congress and the Executive branch would have more time to concentrate on actual delegated responsibilities, and a significant degree of liberty would be restored.

When the modern day TEA Party was formed, the idea was simple. TEA Party was a simple statement by the grass roots of America that we have been "Taxed Enough Already". TEA Party is giving loud and clear voice to the conservative argument that the power of government to tax is very limited and that government has far exceeded that authority. It is time to roll back both the taxation and the excesses of federal government that those taxes support.

U is for Uniformed Military Service

No single group of Americans has withstood the lack of understanding and disrespect of the American people as have those who, through choice or universal draft, served to defend the country from all enemies foreign and domestic. Those who have served honorably in any branch of our armed forces have earned the enduring respect of every citizen of the nation. Unfortunately, many who have not served do not understand the debt owed to those who have served. Most who have served refuse to demand the respect they deserve.

First and foremost, military service requires the individual to surrender a number of individual "rights". For example, freedom of speech is sharply curtailed, freedom of association is limited, freedom from search and seizure is nearly eliminated, and service members are subject to a separate code of military justice. There are no guarantees for the members during their period of service and no assurance that they will not be injured or killed. They are separated from friends and families for extended periods, frequently exposed to the most difficult living conditions, and required to perform tasks at their own peril. The compensation they are provided, when compared to the hours they are required to serve, is minimal and, in some instances, embarrassing. When service members need to apply for and subsist their families using "food stamps" we should all be embarrassed.

Yet they come and serve. Most serve because of a sense of duty. Some serve as a means of improving their lot in life and gaining new opportunity to move up in the economic chain. Regardless of the reason, they do serve and through that service they earn our respect and deserve our support.

A military fighting man is only as good as the training and equipment provided. The best equipment in the world will not make a poorly trained soldier an effective warrior. Similarly, a well-trained individual with a well-honed warrior spirit will not survive long in conflict without the proper equipment. Unfortunately, training and equipment are expensive and are a continuing cost. People leave the service and new people need to be trained. Equipment wears out or becomes obsolete and needs to be replaced. Research and development is expensive and does not always provide desired results. Changes in the political make-up of the world require revisions in both training and equipment to prepare for new threats or new areas of operations. Our service members deserve the very best training, equipment and logistical support we can provide.

Ours is a military of "citizen soldiers". We ask them to serve understanding that they are and will always remain citizens first. They have every expectation to enjoy the same benefits of citizenship as any other individual, including the opportunity to have families and some level of life outside military service. To that end, we have an obligation to make sure that the needs of military families are met. As a nation, in return for active service we should be willing to ensure proper housing for families, sufficient compensation to afford the needs of the family, and a safe, caring environment to nurture and protect the family while the member is absent on duty. The family is "in service" just as certainly as the actual military member and deserves the same support and respect we owe that member.

Military service is a contract between an individual and the people of the country that individual serves. Our government serves as our contracting agent. It is imperative that every part of the agreement is executed properly and fully. It is also imperative that any promise made, either in writing or otherwise, by our government, is faithfully honored. Any individual who experiences injury, in the line of duty, deserves proper medical attention so long as care may be necessary and as complete as may be required to resolve the injury or properly support the individual. Petty squabbles over who pays for post-service treatment or who decides what is or is not service related, all to the detriment of the service member, are inconsistent with the concept of service with honor. The system of post-service medical care needs to be based on a clearly demonstrated need that defaults in favor of the individual, as determined by an independent third party, if necessary, and provides the care appropriate to the injured. When a military member signs the contract for service they do not demand full disclosure, in detail, of how and what will be provided and it is fully inappropriate for our government to try to minimize responsibility after the fact. The contract the individual signs requires them to "Obey all orders". Why should they expect any less of the agents of the government with whom they contracted?

There is a general understanding that military personnel, deployed to a region or area of conflict, will be armed and equipped to protect themselves and to execute the mission they are assigned. Since September 11, 2001 the direct threat to uniformed personnel carrying out duties "in garrison" or at facilities not normally considered hazardous have come under attack and have been ill equipped to defend themselves. We have trained our personnel to protect themselves and others around them and then refused to allow them to be properly equipped to use that training. We are at war, even if our national leadership has difficulty coming to grips with that reality. It is time to properly train and arm our military personnel at home and abroad to ensure their own self-protection. As a start point, every Officer and Non-Commissioned officer (grade E-5 and above) should be required to carry a side arm any time they are in uniform and carrying out their assigned duties.

V is for Veterans Programs and Support

Ours is a nation whose defense is placed in the hands of "citizen soldiers". From our very beginning, the time of settlements and colonies, it has been the individual citizen rising to the call to arms for the defense of home and neighbors that has safeguarded the rights and liberties of all. While we have placed total reliance in our "citizen soldiers", we have not always been faithful to the promises we have made to them.

During our struggle in the Revolution, the failure of our national government to properly feed, house, clothe, arm, and otherwise support the army and navy is a story of great dedication and perseverance by individuals. It is also probable repeated acts of divine intervention offsetting a shameful record of neglect and fear on the part of elected political leadership. Far too often similar behavior, albeit on a somewhat lesser scale, has been the hallmark of our treatment of our national protectors once immediate need has passed.

The enlistment or commissioning of any individual for service in the armed forces is a matter of formal contract between the government and that individual. The contract contains both implicit and implied obligations for both the individual and the government. In the recruiting process, the recruiting official is an agent of the government and the offerings and promises made, part of the reasons the individual agrees to the military commitment, need to be honored. The bottom line has to be "Don't make any promises you cannot keep and keep all promises that you make" The citizens who serve the nation deserve no more and no less.

Part of serving in the military is the associated risk of injury or death as the result of duties or combat action. The enlistee understands the risk and so should the government. In cases of death the government has an obligation to care for the family left behind and should do so with promptness, dignity, and completeness. In the event of injury, the government has the moral obligation to restore

197

the individual to complete health or as close to that state as medical practice will allow. In addition, the government has the obligation to provide continuing support for any injury not fully resolved throughout the life of the soldier, if necessary. Providing medical care for veterans injured in the line of duty is a cost of national defense and not some other line item in the budget. While it might be easier for government to deal with veterans issues through a separate Department and disassociate the cost of veteran's care from the defense budget, they cannot be unlinked. For existing veterans who were drafted into service and had no say in the decision, there is a clear responsibility for that continuing care. The nation demanded their service and now the nation is responsible to take care of those who deserve that care. In the current situation of an all-volunteer force, it will not take long for those volunteers to become few in number when they realize that they carry all of the risk associated with service but are granted few of the promised benefits.

While the apparent general lack of concern is unconscionable, it is made even worse by a government that, at every turn, actively fights to limit responsibility for any injury or sickness that might be related to service. Asking a soldier to fight for his country and then have to fight with his country for help is just about as poor a circumstance as possible. Conducting extensive studies to determine if an injury or illness is real in the face of the existing evidence presented by the number of individuals affected is unacceptable. Spending years to establish beyond any doubt that some government action may be the specific cause of a wide-spread illness defies logic. When a significant number of combat veterans display similar symptoms, the problem is real and deserves attention, not a study to find out who or what caused the problem before appropriate and required assistance is offered.

Not all veterans deserve the support of the nation. There are some who, through their own misbehavior, were separated from service under other than honorable conditions. Because of the terms of their enlistment contract they are properly denied most of the benefits extended to veterans. However, an individual who was injured in the line of duty, regardless of the nature of discharge, earned the contracted benefits of medical care for that injury. A misconduct discharge , not related to the injuries sustained or illness incurred in the line of duty, cannot and should not reduce or relieve the government responsibility to provide necessary continuing care.

If the citizens of our nation cannot or will not provide for the health and welfare of those who served to protect the nation, what exactly do we stand for?

W is for Welfare Programs

There is a specific need to understand the difference between the concepts of "Welfare" (providing for the most needy) and "entitlement" (a legislated "right" created by government). In this section welfare will be the subject of interest.

It is in the very nature of conservatives to care for those in need and to provide for those who are unable to provide for themselves. It is also in the nature of conservatives to hold in small regard those who are capable of providing for themselves but who choose to rely on the charity of others or the largess of government.

Because two basic elements of the conservative character are self-reliance and personal responsibility, it is reasonably easy to separate out those in need of our assistance and those who would choose to rely on our good nature rather than take care of themselves. Conservatives will always take care of the former and do our best to encourage and guide the latter to a more responsible life style.

The time honored American ideal of parents caring for children and children caring for parents has suffered heavily with the purposeful decline of the concept of family and the eradication of family values. In the past, when the nominal family included both a mother and father, at home, attending to the needs of the family and the children, a strong bond and uniting force existed. Of course not all families were perfect and the "Ozzie and Harriet" example was a bit on the extreme side. But families were strong and the lasting ability of the family to take care of itself was instrumental in our society.

One of the most immediate results and clear indicators of the down side of the welfare programs (from the Conservative point of view) is the degradation of the American family and the resultant number of children who are forced to grow up in an ever challenging world without the support of two parents and substantive role models. The rise of the number of young men who are undereducated and unemployed, leading to disrespect for traditional values and for each other, has created a near epidemic of tragedy in the country. For a Progressive, the current state of affairs is a desired condition because it supports their agenda of racial division, class division, and continued reliance on government support. Unfortunately for those who are "beneficiaries" of the Progressive programs, the support never meets the promises and the overall lifestyle and economic conditions are never improved. The individuals who chose to accept Progressive welfare solutions as the basis for their lifestyle now suffer the consequences of that choice. Unfortunately, so do all others because of the spill-over into general society.

There is a way out of the chaos and destruction of life that has been created by an unfettered welfare state. It will not be an easy path and it is one fraught with political hazard. We should expect strong opposition to change from those who benefit most from continuing the existing system. The Progressives are creating a large base of dependency voters among those enjoying the benefits of the system who are satisfied with their lives and the future they are building for their children. That said, among this group we will also find those who strongly support change. Individuals who understand that the future is theirs if they are willing to meet the challenges, work hard, and take the risks will certainly opt out of the welfare system. Those mothers and fathers who want more for their children will be ready for positive change, as are young adults who recognize that almost any positive change is better than continuing in the life of gangs, violence, and poverty that they most certainly face. The process to change that outcome will depend on dedication of conservatives to bring real change and to educate the people as to the value and benefit of change to them. The road to success will not be easy and the risk of setback is high. That is all the more reason to dedicate ourselves to the success of our proposal

There are several elements that must be included in any program that will move individuals from welfare support to self-dependence.

1. Education to achieve success in the society as we know it today must be provided and strengthened. We cannot simply deny existing benefits to individuals who want to educate themselves to move off of welfare. The Conservative program must continue the support until the individual is ready and able to be self-supporting. Programs like "No-Child-Left-Behind' and "Common Core" are not the answer because they perpetuate a system that does not focus on real outcomes for real people.

2. Incentives to become self–dependent must be greater than the incentives to remain on welfare. Through use of actual "means testing" and effective monitoring, exiting benefits would be provided only at the minimal level. In addition, the work requirement and total time that benefits will be provided also need to be a part of the program. To that end, the Conservative approach must include a sliding scale of benefits that encourages an individual to seek work without risk of loss of all benefits or a reduction in life-style.

3. A positive disincentive for the birth of children out of wedlock needs to be created and implemented. Conservatives need to be more concerned about the future of these children than the "cost" of having them on the welfare rolls. If we are firm in our belief that terminating a fetus before birth is wrong, we must also understand that birth of a child destined to a life of poverty and hardship is just as wrong. If children born out of wedlock are to become effective wards of the state through continuing welfare program benefits, then the state needs to make sure that their "wards" are properly raised and have an equal chance at success.

4. We must develop a short term support program that is always available for those who, through circumstances of life, find themselves in need of help. This program must be short in length, strong in support for a return to self-dependence, and not susceptible to expansion or benefit creep. We cannot end welfare by establishing another "compassionate" program to replace it.

5. The Conservative solution must include a means of disallowing welfare families from congregating in closed communities or neighborhoods that become self-perpetuating. Families and individuals receiving support from the government must become an integral part of the community. If society wants to end welfare as a drain on our resources and a deterrent to real economic growth, we will have to accept that all not of our neighbors will be as well off as we are and that some may need a bit more help than others in assimilating into our communities.

The single most important area for Conservatives to concentrate on in the effort to correct the negative impact created by the Progressive driven welfare state and to restore hope and promise to the millions of Americans trapped in that environment will be the nation's inner cities. For far too long, we have allowed and perhaps encouraged those of the lowest economic strata to migrate into our cities, create communities of common despair, avoid the demands of society for self-dependence, and ultimately become safe harbors for criminals and those who would prey on others. The Progressive central planning mantra that moving workers into the major urban area would also draw meaningful employment has never proven true. Instead, we have trapped people in cities with no opportunity for meaningful work, failing education systems, and a growing need of government support. That approach, with all it's identified failing precepts, needs to be reversed.

Only when the existing welfare state is completely eliminated and a more appropriate program of essential short term support established will we be able to collectively seek the American Dream and enjoy the benefits of that outcome.

Chapter 18 Wrapping It All Up For Now

The primary objective of this missive is to awaken and inspire the large number of fellow Americans who are, deep down inside, real conservatives. My intent was to make this a voyage of discovery through which realization replaced doubt and courage supplanted fear of condemnation. My desire was to awaken so many conservative voices that mine would be lost in a sea of positive American exceptionalism voiced by untold numbers of American Political conservatives.

You are not alone and you need not fear. Accept that, as you begin to enter the stage of expressed opinion, the Progressives and "America faulters" will do everything in their power to discredit you personally and attack you as the messenger. Please remember that employing "bully" tactics is a way of life for Progressives (while they accuse everyone else of being bullies) and that they will not mount fact based arguments to counter your positions. They cannot succeed in shutting you down if you will only muster the courage to prevail. There is great strength to be gained from the play yard wisdom found in "Sticks and stones may break my bones but words will never harm me". Perseverance pays and you and all of the rest of us will be successful when we refuse to yield the language, the podium, or the field of dreams and ideas. After all, we are right and they are wrong. How much more simple and direct can a call to arms be?

Keep the faith that America and its base conservative values will continue to be the positive example for the world. You can make that happen. I trust you and I have faith in you.

Xcept for the disbursements for services and responsibilities as set forth in the Constitution

Y are we, as taxpayers and citizens, allowing our government to spend the

Zillions of our hard earned dollars they do on their pet projects and to buy votes to stay in office (to spend more money)???

Made in the USA
Coppell, TX
29 July 2020